RHYMES
OF A RAVER

TRIBUTE TO A CASTLE OF SALVAGED SOULS

RICHARD DAVID COMSTOCK
INTRODUCTION BY *S & SF PHILLIPS*

DEDICATION

Richard David Comstock dedicated this book, most appropriately,

"To that rare gem, a Friend, that shines through the dismal
fog of despair with a transcendent lustre that warms and
whispers courage to a heart wearied of its misery. To Mrs.
D.E.D., who is such a friend, is this book dedicated."

I was unable to locate any additional information about, "Mrs. D.E.D," but she was probably a kindly member of the Greystone nursing or administrative staff. In the final section, "My Sojourn at Greystone," Mr. Comstock makes another dedication of this book, his "first literary contribution, to the public." He would be deeply saddened to learn that old Greystone, his "refuge mercy-marked," is now just a memory, but pleased that his literary contribution has finally been made available to the public, over 87 years after it was first published in the Print Shop of the Industrial Building.

I dedicate this reprint to my Father, Dr. Jacob Forman, DDS, who served in the Greystone Hospital Dental Clinic from April, 1960 until his death in April, 1972, when I was 15 years old. I never had the opportunity to thank him for his service to our Nation in the US Army during World War II, or to his patients at Greystone as a dental surgeon, so I would like to take this opportunity to say thanks Dad, for a lifetime of hard work, dedication, and sacrifice. Numerous members of the *Greatest Generation*, like my Dad, were first generation Americans who performed their patriotic duty during that terrible war, fought to keep America and our world safe and free from tyranny, often at the cost of life and limb. Hat tip to one and all, along with a heartfelt thank you, to the dedicated staff of old Greystone, who served the mentally and physically challenged, as well as the outcast and helpless orphans and elderly, for over a century. That legacy of service continues, in the newly rebuilt Greystone Park Psychiatric Hospital, Morris Plains, New Jersey.

FOREWORD BY R.D.C

In the first place this is not a book of poetry but of rhymes. In the next place I am not a writer. The rhymes herein are plain chronicles of things that have really happened and are not the result of an inspired poet's thoughts.

To me there belongs no credit for the contents of this book. I only wrote what was enacted and performed by those about me here. They are the real writers.

And if some thought in my little forest of rhymes be of some benefit to some person who reads them, not to R. D. C., the interpreter, should the praise be rendered, but to those connected with this institution where I was granted the knowledge and insight into the most supreme benefits to humanity imaginable.

Greystone Park may well he christened a "Castle of Salvaged Souls." For so often here an almost new body must be builded around an undeveloped spirit ere it reaches the realization that a soul is existent. And it seems to me that it is only fair to those of Greystone Park for me to state plainly that it was here that I found I had a soul and could ever hope to lead a happy, useful. contented life, rebuilt in mind and body.

This is my first and last book. Soon I shall go out into the great, new, glorious world of hopeful achievement and endeavor. I shall plunge into my horticultural work and engineering again. I have confidence in myself now, plenty of it. I am happy and grateful to Greystone Park where so much has been done for· me, as for countless others. On your way little book.

Morris Plains, New Jersey.

ACKNOWLEDGMENT BY R.D.C.

"I am indebted to all those who have made it possible for me to publish this book, to those who so govern Greystone Park that it inspires so many of my rhymes; to the Board of Managers; to the Commissioner of Institutions and Agencies of New Jersey; to our Superintendent, whose sincerity and interest for his patients is splendid, indeed; to the Senior Resident Physician who, bearing aloft the indestructible principles of Occupational Therapy, is plowing a mighty furrow in the weedy fields of mental and nervous ailments; to every doctor at Greystone, but particularly to those who at some time or another during my stay treated me; to the technicians of the laboratory; to the supervisors; to the business office employees; to every single employee who helps in any way to make and keep Greystone Park what it is.

To our Social Service Department; to our Department of Physical Education; to all my fellow patients amongst whom I made my comeback; to the patients employed in the Print Shop who aided in publishing this book; to the X-Ray Department; to all the employees of the Hydrotherapy Dept; to the dentists; to the grand old young man of the trees and things horticultural, who helped me so much when I was shaky last winter; to my secretary, assistant. and friend L. S. F., who helped me so much to prepare this bundle of rhymes; and last but not by any means least, to the Manager of the Print Shop who backed me up and helped me give this book to the world outside, and to the employees who unselfishly gave of their own time that the work might be completed better and quicker.

To all of these and many more do I offer acknowledgment of help and inspiration.

Richard David Comstock

ACKNOWLEDGMENT

I discovered this little book in 2014, just after I heard the sad news about the impending demolition of the old Kirkbride buildings of Greystone Park Psychiatric Hospital. Unfortunately, despite the best efforts of John Huebner, the members of the Board of *Preserve Greystone,* and the concerned citizens who devoted much time and effort to save these historically important buildings, demolition was complete by the spring of 2015. I would like to thank Mr. Huebner and the folks who fought so tenaciously, for their efforts to save the remainder of the buildings and for the informative website, still standing, that provides so many lovely photos of Greystone through the years, as well as an interesting time line and history (www.preservegreystone.com). A special thanks to members of *Preserve Greystone,* Advisory Board, Ms. Sue Schmidt, Preservationist, and Founder and President of the historic Ayres/Knuth Farm Foundation in Denville, NJ (http://ayresknuth.org/), and Ms. Margaret Westfield, R.A., Historic Architect, Partner at Westfield Architects & Preservation Consultants (http://www.wa-pc.com/), for their assistance and moral support.

Ms. Susan Vigilante, President, Morris County Historical Society and daughter of the Reverend Joseph E. Walsh, Chaplain of Greystone Hospital from 1914 until his death in 1962, has provided information, as well as invaluable moral support, from the beginning of this project. The Reverend Walsh also served as pastor of the Presbyterian Church of Morris Plains from 1928 to 1961. Mr. Comstock dedicated his first rhyme, "The Man of God," to Reverend Walsh, who was the first "customer" to purchase this book at the Greystone Print Shop.

When I made the decision to reprint *Rhymes,* I was assisted in my research efforts by Ms. Cheryl Turkington, Librarian, *Morristown & Morris Township Library, North Jersey History & Genealogy Center.* Ms. Turkington provided invaluable assistance, by locating several copies of *The Psychogram*, Greystone's patient and staff newsletter, unavailable on the internet, as well as copies of the *New Jersey State Hospital Annual Reports,* beginning with a report from 1908. In the July, 1961 edition of *The Psychogram,* I learned my Dad, Dr. Jacob Forman, DDS, "joined the staff of Greystone on April 4, 1960." I also learned Greystone added their first resident dentist, Dr. William G. Sharp, DDS, in 1914, according to the *Thirty-Ninth Annual Report of the Managers and Officers of the New Jersey State Hospital at Morris Plains, For the Year Ending October 31st, 1914.* Shortly before publication, Mr. James Lewis, Head of the *North Jersey History and Genealogy Center, Morristown and Morris Township Library*, kindly granted permission to use the lovely photo of the original Victorian style Administration Building, for the cover of this reprint.

A very special thank you goes to my friend and mentor, survival fiction author, Mr. Lloyd Tackitt. In addition to providing guidance for my various writing efforts, Lloyd located an article about Mr. Richard David Comstock in the July 24, 1930, evening edition of the Queens Borough New York newspaper, *Daily Star.* He also found an advertisement in the same newspaper, of Mr. Comstock's horticultural services business in Flushing, New York, *United Landscape Engineers and Foresters,* placed on July 26 and July 27, 1930, shortly after his release from Greystone Hospital. Mr. Glendon Haddix of *Streetlight Graphics*, created this attractive and dignified cover, as well as formatted the reprint of the book, which was a challenge. He has done an outstanding job and I believe, Mr. Comstock would have been pleased with our humble efforts to re-present his *Rhymes.*

I must include a special acknowledgment of Mr. Robert Love, who became like a father to me, from 1976 until his death in 2007. Mr. Love was a veteran of the US Army and his stepson, Lieutenant Colonel Theodore Brostrom, deserves an especially honorable mention for his service in the US Army for twenty-two years, including a tour of duty in Vietnam in the 101st Airborne Division. Teddy served God and country selflessly, with a spirit of generosity and a brilliant sense of humor, until Non-Hodgkins Lymphoma ended his life on earth, in 2012.

Lastly, thanks to my husband Steve, who assisted with the preparation of our *Introduction* and all necessary research, as well as for the wisdom and inspiration he brings to our projects. Steve is co-editor of our first book, *Wisdom from King Alfred's Middle Earth – Books Most Necessary to Know.*

TABLE OF CONTENTS

Introduction...1
The Man Of God...19
Requiem Of The Pines..22
Preface In Rhyme...25
The Girl From Home...31
Nobody's Sweetheart...34
The Gutter Takes Back Its Own....................................36
I Just Noticed..39
Nurse Malone..43
Salutation To A Brave Spirit...45
Soliloquies..47
The Portrait...52
Knight Of The Jangling Keys.......................................56
That Little Cart Of Books..59
The Symphony...62
A Sister Of Mercy..66
That Chap They Call Mcnuff.......................................69
Gebertig–A Brother To Men...72
In The House Of Kadji Smoo.......................................75
A Thorobred..79
Guardian Of The Night...80
Valley Of Passing Men..82
The Whim Of A Dancing Girl......................................84
Over The Hill To Nunn's...88
Requiescat In Pace...90
The Dreamer..92

The Come-Back 94

Ode To One Of Our Little Ones 98

Adolph The Barber 100

Memories 102

Song Of A Dizzy One 104

Let This Be Nameless 107

The Guarded Ones 109

Always Like This 112

Omnipotence Divine 114

Through The Shadows 117

The World Shall Know 120

Laird Of The Lance 123

The Low-Brow 125

La Longue Traverse 127

The Crystal In The Blaze 129

Laugh With Joy Awhile 132

The Moth And I 133

The Ship Of State 137

The Hard Riding Kid Of Bar T. 140

Greystone's Holy Night 148

Thanks To Commissioner Ellis 153

One Of Life's Tragedies 156

Thou Art Known 161

The Trail Of The Little Red Ball 165

A Tale Of Long Ago 167

Life 172

Love's Memory 173

The Fool 175

Lifters Of The Veil 177

A Little Kiddie Waiting For Her Dad On Number Four 179

Christmas At Greystone Park 181

Just A Rhyming Raver On North-Three-One 183

Obsessional 186

I'm Telling The World That I'm One 190

Memoirs Of The Dawn 195

The Passing Of A Rose 201

To Marcia 203

Cap O' The Sail Patrol 204

A Father Speaks 207

Song Of The Bars 210

Salutation To A Brother's Keeper 212

Just Coo – Coo 214

Veriliy, You Shall Find Peace 217

Good Advice 219

The Mascot Of Greystone Park 221

The Doctor's Prayer 223

Leaving It Up To You 225

That Li'l Forget-Me-Not 227

One Of Our Girls 231

Devine 233

Angel Of Whispering Hope 235

Salutation Ad Infinitum 237

Calling 239

We Patients Wonder 242

That's Scotty 244

Opening Of The Shell 246

Greetings To Governor Larson 247

And Last 249

My Sojourn At Greystone Park By R.D.C 252

About The Presenters 260

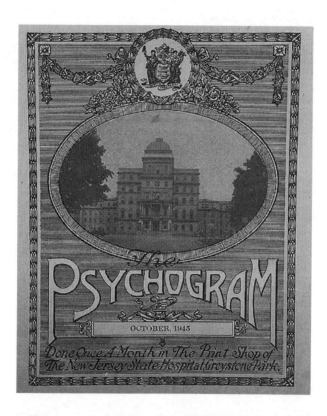

Diversional Therapy- Bookbinding Department, 1919

INTRODUCTION

None of us can imagine the fear, loneliness, and sense of foreboding Richard David Comstock must have felt on his first day at Greystone, one day in August, 1929. A broken man, just under 35 years of age, in *Rhymes of a Raver,* we learn he was suffering from years of alcohol abuse and some type of lung disorder. In his *FOREWARD,* Mr. Comstock tells us it was in Greystone Park, where he found he "had a soul and could ever hope to lead a happy, useful, contented life, rebuilt in mind and body." After reading his "little forest of rhymes," that relate bits and pieces of his life experiences, including those at Greystone, we learn about the professional, compassionate, and humane treatment he received in that old hospital, and how he found his *soul.* He reverently refers to Greystone as,

> "this institution where I was granted the knowledge
> and insight into the most supreme benefits to humanity
> imaginable."

In his *ACKNOWLEDGMENT,* Mr. Comstock thanks an extensive list of doctors, staff, and administrators of Greystone Park, who made it possible for him to publish this book, including, the Board of Managers, Commissioner of Institutions and Agencies of New Jersey, and Senior Resident Physician, "who, bearing aloft the indestructible principles of Occupational Therapy, is plowing a mighty furrow in the weedy fields of mental and nervous ailments." He goes on to thank, "every doctor at Greystone," including technicians of the Laboratory, supervisors, business office employees, the Social Service Department, the X-Ray Department, and so on.

Rhymes, gives the reader a little window into one patient's experience

1

and perspective of Greystone, circa 1929 to 1930. It also gave me a whole new appreciation for that old, very tired looking hospital I remember, during the late 1960s and early 70s. This book makes the reader stop and think about what might have happened to Mr. Comstock, had it not been for this venerable institution, created just over 50 years before he arrived. Our *Raver,* could have ended his life in prison or in a literal "gutter." The dedicated professionals who pioneered treatments for the mentally ill, and built this, and other similar "asylums," created places of refuge and healing for countless numbers of helpless souls, abandoned by society. Today, their efforts remain mostly unknown and unappreciated by many, including unfortunately, by our legislators and other officials.

Throughout history, there have been trailblazers whose zeal, dedication, and tenacity enlightened and changed the world, one brilliant individual at a time, in all areas of human endeavor. In the field of science, for example, the name Albert Einstein (1879-1955), 20th century physicist known for his *Theory of Relativity,* has become synonymous with *genius.* Sigmund Freud (1856-1939), founder of *psychoanalysis* during the 1890s, remains a "pop culture icon" for the professions of psychology and psychiatry, and his method of clinical treatment is still in use today. Most early advocates for the mentally ill remain unsung heroes, despite their significant contributions to the many noble professions that fall under the umbrella of *mental health.* A few notable mental health professionals include, Dr. Francis Sumner (1895-1954), the first African-American to earn a Ph.D. in psychology in 1920, and referred to as, "The Father of Black Psychology" (http://www.aaregistry.org/historic_events/view/francis-c-sumner-born). Dr. Sumner worked closely with Dr. G. Stanley Hall (1844-1924), "founder of organized psychology as a science and profession," as well as a national leader of educational reform, during his time at Clark University (http://muskingum.edu/~psych/psycweb/history/hall.htm).

Dorothea Dix (1802-1887), selfless champion and, "educator and social reformer whose devotion to the welfare of the mentally ill led to widespread international reforms," was instrumental in ending the cruel and inhumane treatment of the mentally ill, prevalent during the 19th century and earlier, in America and abroad (http://www.biography.com/people/dorothea-dix-9275710). Her tireless efforts at lobbying Congress for funds to construct humane institutions for the mentally ill, as well as the blind and deaf, facilitated the establishment of psychiatric hospitals throughout America and eventually, Europe. Dr. Thomas Story Kirkbride (1809-1883), founding member, *Association of Medical Superintendents of American Institutions for the Insane*, forerunner of the *American Psychiatric Association*, formed a friendship with Ms. Dix based on their common interests and goals. Their efforts resulted in the establishment of asylums constructed, based on their innovative ideas for the most effective and humane way to treat the mentally ill. The first hospital constructed on the "Kirkbride Plan," opened in Trenton, New Jersey in 1848 (http://www. kirkbridebuildings.com/about/kirkbride.html). The State Lunatic Asylum at Morris Plains, the future Greystone Park Psychiatric Hospital, opened its doors to 342 patients in 1877, built to alleviate the overcrowding in Trenton State Hospital (http://www.preservegreystone.org/history.html).

Although Greystone began experiencing overcrowding by 1895, during the early years, it must have been a pleasant place with its magnificent Kirkbride buildings, well-appointed Victorian furnishings and decor, "state of the art" humane therapies, lovely grounds, and dedicated staff. Unfortunately, those "glory days" were starting to wane by the 1950s, but when Mr. Comstock was admitted as a patient in 1929, the hospital was still a sanctuary for the chronically mentally ill and a place of refuge and healing for patients, like Mr. Comstock, who could be rehabilitated and released to enjoy life once again. By the 1970s and 1980s, when deinstitutionalization began to take effect and government funding for psychiatric facilities was significantly reduced, the once stately hospital fell into disrepair and patient care seriously suffered, despite the best efforts of dedicated staff.

In 2008, the remaining patients were moved out of the crumbling old hospital into the new facility currently in use and in that same year, a dedicated group of preservationists, environmentalists, and concerned citizens, founded *Preserve Greystone*, led by Mr. John Huebner. A "statewide public awareness campaign" to save the remaining Kirkbride buildings and grounds was launched, but unfortunately, ended in the spring of 2015, when this New Jersey "architectural treasure" was demolished. In a "Letter to the Editor," July 9, 2015, in the website, *Tap into Morristown,* Mr. Huebner, President of *Preserve Greystone*, reminds us, "Numerous examples exist of Kirkbride Buildings in other states (some of lower quality, and in far worse shape than our Greystone) that now serve as community centers, mixed use commercial/residential villages, and wildly popular tourist destinations" (https://www.tapinto.net/towns/morristown/categories/news/articles/letter-by-john-huebner-president-preserve-greyst#). He leaves us with the somber thought that the destruction of Kirkbride Greystone, "an irreplaceable public heirloom that was built to last forever," is not only "an irretrievable loss for this generation and countless future ones," but also "an affront to the generation that built it."

One year after Greystone was demolished, Rusty Tagliareni and Christina Mathews, published, *Greystone Park Psychiatric Hospital*, for the book series, *Images of America*, (Arcadia Publishing, 2016) that provides an impressive pictorial history of the hospital from its inception to unfortunate demolition. The book also presents a brilliant "Introduction" by Robert Kirkbride, where he reminds us, on page 8,

> "Kirkbride hospitals are among our nation's most compelling social innovations, providing shelter for the unfortunate as part of the broader public good and a more level playing field for the pursuit of happiness as an inalienable right. Destruction of such products of human care and skill, willful or not, is not merely wasteful; it is hubristic and nonsensical."

Hopefully, these admonitions will remind our public officials, with the responsibility of caring for America's treasured historic buildings, to take that responsibility seriously and act as good stewards of America's architectural heritage. Every time an historically significant building is demolished, a part of our social and cultural heritage is also lost. Our generation would do well to heed this warning from an African proverb, "As you do for your ancestors, your children will do for you" (https://blog.genealogybank.com/101-genealogy-proverbs-family-sayings-from-around-the-world.html).

Fortunately, other Kirkbride buildings were successfully saved, as was St. Elizabeth's Hospital, opened in 1855 as the *Government Hospital for the Insane*, currently considered for renovation. Planning is underway to renovate and repurpose the campus, in the Anacostia neighborhood of Washington, DC, for use by the Federal Government. One of the "Development Objectives" of this project, is to "provide a federal workplace of world-class design," and if successful, the result will be another Kirkbride building preserved, to honor America's 19th century architectural heritage, into our 21st century (https://www.gsa.gov/portal/category/100799).

At the time of this writing, The National Building Museum in Washington, DC, is featuring an exhibit, "Architecture of an Asylum: St. Elizabeths 1852-2017" (http://www.nbm.org/). Sarah Leavitt, Curator of the Museum and filmmaker Sarah Mondale, presented the film, *Asylum,* on June 13, 2017,

> "that takes a detailed look at the history of St. Elizabeths to debate the question of whether deinstitutionalization has proved an overall failure, leaving more patients homeless than are mainstreamed into society, and if the time has come to reintroduce the asylum as a place of therapy and benign confinement."

A few years ago, I began to reminisce about my childhood in New Jersey and to search for information about Greystone Park Hospital, where my Dad, Dr. Jacob Forman, served in the dental clinic for 12 years, from 1960 to 1972. I started with the internet and what I found was quite interesting, including information that the legendary American singer-song writer Woody Guthrie, was a patient at Greystone from 1956 to 1961, during his battle with Huntington's disease. His son, Arlo Guthrie, made frequent visits to Greystone during that time and Woody was also visited by another, now legendary singer song-writer, Bob Dylan, in 1960.

The most interesting discovery, however, was this little book, *Rhymes of a Raver,* written while Mr. Richard David Comstock was a patient at Greystone and published in, "The Print Shop." Thankfully, Mr. Comstock had the book copyrighted in May,1930, by the Library of Congress. I became fascinated with the idea that a book could be written and published by someone, while a patient, in a so-called "mental institution." I continued to search the internet to see if I could find other similar books, but this was the only book of its kind, I was able to locate. To the best of my knowledge, *Rhymes* may possibly be the only book written and printed in any psychiatric institution in America, accepted for copyright. Finding an actual copy of the book, however, was challenging and I initially attempted to borrow one of the only known copies still in existence, from the Morris Township

Library. I attempted to utilize the interlibrary loan process between Morris Township and our local library, but unfortunately, Morris Township only had one original copy from 1930, in fragile condition, so it could not be loaned to any other library.

I was unable to travel to New Jersey, so I continued to search for a copy I could borrow, as this book was out of print and could not be purchased. Fortunately, the Library of Congress agreed to send their copy to our local library, with the caveat that the book remain in the library until it was returned to Washington, DC. When the book arrived, I carefully made a paper copy and next attempted to determine if it could be legally reprinted and made available to the public, as Mr. Comstock originally intended. After conducting extensive research on copyright law, I discovered the *Catalog of Copyright Entries (CCE)* on the Copyright Office website, www.copyright. gov. The information provided by the United States Copyright Office, in *Circular 22.0213, Works First Published or Copyrighted Between January 1, 1923 and December 31, 1949, But Not Renewed*, states the following,

> "If a work was first published or copyrighted between January 1, 1923, and December 31, 1949, it is important to determine whether the copyright was renewed during the last (28th) year of the first term of the copyright. This can be done by searching the Copyright Office records or catalogs as explained previously. If no renewal registration was made, copyright protection expired permanently at the end of the 28th year from the year it was first secured."

The 28th year after Mr. Comstock received his copyright in 1930, was 1958, and after thoroughly searching all copyright renewals for that year, as well as several years prior, under the name Comstock, I determined this book has been in the "public domain" since 1958, as I could find no evidence that Mr. Comstock renewed his copyright. I then made the decision, to "give this book to the world outside," as stated in the book's original *ACKNOWLEDGMENT*. In *FOREWARD*, he refers to Greystone, as a *Castle of Salvaged Souls*, and tells us, "The rhymes herein are plain chronicles of things that have really happened and are not the result of an inspired poet's thoughts." In the space of 83 rhymes, Mr. Comstock presents bits and pieces of his experience at Greystone and a few of his life adventures and "escapades."

The Print Shop, where this book was created, was housed in Greystone's "Industrial Building," opened in 1915 as part of their "diversional occupation" program, or what we today refer to as, "occupational therapy." In *Legislative Documents, Forty-First Annual Report of the Managers and Officers of the New Jersey State Hospital at Morris Plains, For the Year Ending October 31, 1916, p. 37*, "Diversional Occupation," we read,

> "Since the opening of the Industrial Building two years ago, very satisfactory results have been obtained in the application of the fundamental principles of diversional occupation as a means of treating patients afflicted with mental and nervous diseases."

Interesting as well,

> "In the printing department and bookbindery the results have been constantly positive, and the development of this industry has been very progressive, both from a medical and an economical standpoint. Patients who have been in this institution for a long time without having contributed anything towards their maintenance have been able to do an order of work in the printing department which, if justly evaluated, would be greatly in excess of actual cost of their maintenance."

In addition to providing patients with the opportunity to participate in woodcraft, sewing, construction and maintenance of the facilities, bookbinding and printing, gardening, carpentry, as well as a myriad of amusements, another early innovation of, "diversional occupation" that employed the Print Shop, was the creation of *The Psychogram,* to bring the patient,

> "in closer touch with his friends and relatives the publication of a monthly magazine was started July 1ˢᵗ (1916). The title PSYCHOGRAM, which was given to the magazine, has a significant connotation, and is intended to

convey to the general public in a very modest way the unusual capabilities of people who are unfortunately afflicted
with mental disorders. The object of PSYCHOGRAM is
set forth in its editorial column as follows: 'THE PSYCH-
GRAM is published chiefly for the purpose of arousing a
spirit of congeniality among all those who are residents
of this institution; to encourage intellectual and moral
improvements in the personalities of all those who have
occasion to read it; to bring cheer and gladness to patients
who are separated from their friends and relatives; and for
the purpose of giving reliable information to friends, relatives and such members of the general public as may be
interested in the conduct and welfare of this large public
charity maintained at Morris Plains for the treatment and
care of persons suffering from the various forms of mental
derangement."

The National Committee for Mental Health Hygiene of New York City,
became a regular contributor, sending articles relating to, "Friends of the
Insane."

"The extra demands made upon the patients for the
production of this publication have not only awakened new
interest in patients possessing literary ability, but have also
helped a great deal to bring out a few more patients who
have had experience as printers before they came to the
institution, or who showed ability in this art and desired
to share somewhat in the glory of this modest publication."

"Modest," perhaps, but *The Psychogram* played a pivotal role in Mr.
Comstock's eventual rehabilitation, when selected by Dr. George B.
McMurray, to write an editorial on a day when the Patient Editor was
absent. He refers to Dr. McMurray in the summary section of *Rhymes*, "My
Sojourn at Greystone,"

"I do not understand what it was nor have I ever asked,
but friends, out there in your great, glistening world of

freedom, from that moment words rushed from my pen *in rhyme*. I wrote the editorial; it pleased him. From that moment I was another person. I hadn't cared much for life up to then but now I was crazy to live. Then in just a few days he placed me in the Print Shop as Manager of "The Psychogram." He gave me a clear rein. He trusted me. He gave me a parole with no restrictions and gave me no orders nor threats."

Mr. Comstock first began publishing his rhymes in *The Psychogram*, and eventually created this book, but more importantly, the inspiration and self-confidence received while working in the Print Shop, gave him a renewed sense of purpose and lease on life. In *ACKNOWLEDGMENT*, he praises, "the indestructible principles of Occupational Therapy." *The National Society for the Promotion of Occupational Therapy*, was founded two years after Greystone opened their Industrial Building, in 1917, and occupational therapy remains today, a critical profession for helping people of all ages to gain or regain critical skills and abilities lost due to various types of physical or mental challenges (http://www.aota.org/About-Occupational-Therapy.aspx).

Throughout *Rhymes*, Mr. Comstock refers to Greystone as a place of refuge and healing. This is apparent in old photos, where we see patients, not only engaged in various forms of therapy and recreation, but also enjoying a clean and attractive work and living environment. A photo of patients working in the Bookbinding Department in 1919, has been added to this reprint, courtesy of *Preserve Greystone*. In the last section of *Rhymes*, he also emphasizes his intension for publishing this book,

> "The world should know of the indescribable good wrought here at Greystone Park. I wish I might give my life to the cause for which Dr. Marcus A. Curry and Dr. George B. McMurray are striving. I have traveled the world, mixed with every type of human, and the divers associations have developed within me a reliable instinct which tells me plainly of sincerity and unselfishness, or indifference and greed, and I tell you readers, that in thirty years of travel never have I met with men who have gained one-half the

good for humanity that these two men have brought about. If you would have told me those first months of my sojourn here that I would be writing poetry and stories that anyone would like to read in two months' time, I would have walked away wondering which one of us two was the crazier."

Mr. Comstock dedicated his first rhyme, "The Man of God," to the Reverend Joseph E. Walsh, Chaplain of Greystone, from 1914 until his death in 1962. The Reverend Walsh also served as Pastor of the Presbyterian Church of Morris Plains, from 1928 to 1961, and was first to purchase this book in the "Print Shop." In this rhyme, we learn that in addition to honoring Reverend Walsh as a "kindly man" with a "brotherly smile," Mr. Comstock pays tribute for his service as a "sincere man of God." He makes an interesting correlation between his time spent "mongst the trees," and his ability to "clearly understand that he was a man of God," as well as comparing the "spirit," "strength," and "calm," of Reverend Walsh, to the "spready oak," "western pine," and "redwood," as follows:

"So like a shady, *spready oak*
His spirit sent its wave
To welcome babies, 'ere they'd spoke
And restful make the grave.

Yes, like a towering *western pine*
His strength swept o'er the sod
Like *redwood* smiling calm at time,
So stood this man of God."

At the end of this first rhyme, there is an additional reference to nature and to his wish, that "some other" *sinner* may be helped by this book,

"You are the first to buy my book,
Wherein I've *sowed the seed*
That I do so much want to brook
Some other sinner's need.

And to me it's a glorious sign
That rhymes of us who plod

On dreary road send first their lines
To sincere man of God."

It is apparent in every rhyme about Greystone, that from his first day in the hospital, Mr. Comstock was carefully guided on his sojourn of healing and rehabilitation. I will not attempt to address every rhyme individually, but highlight a few, particularly interesting or poignant rhymes, but please remember to place them in the context of the year in which they were published, as some references can be considered offensive. Most, however, contain "folksy wisdom" and timeless advice.

His second rhyme, "Requiem of the Pines," is dedicated to his friend and fellow forest fire fighter, Douglas C. Ingram, who served in the Forest Service from 1909 until his death in 1929, in the Camas Creek Fire on August 13, in Chelan National Forest, Washington. Mr. Ingram is honored in, *The Methow Valley Wildland Firefighter Memorial, A Tribute to Wildland Firefighters* (http://www.wlfalwaysremember.org/incident-lists/297-chelan-nf-fires.html). In "Requiem," Mr. Comstock reminisces about a fire he and Mr. Ingram fought together, in Oregon and how he pledges, to "still plug on at saving trees." We also learn Mr. Comstock's lungs were "seared at Paine's," most likely referring to another forest fire they fought together.

In "Preface in Rhyme," Mr. Comstock reveals the primary reason for his admission,

"If one drink on like me they'll fall
And wake betwixt the sullen walls,
With body shaken, mind a mess,
An outcast wreck a helpless pest."

"The Girl from Home," gives us a glimpse of his experience while "hittin" for Khartoum, apparently to do some diamond mining somewhere in the area. In this rhyme, we learn Mr. Comstock recovered from an illness that may have been malaria, but his buddy, "Peg Leg Billy Dunn," did not survive and was laid to rest in a jungle, far away from his native New Jersey. A rhyme likely written before he regained his will to live, "Nobody's Sweetheart," refers to suicide, when he mentions, "death in this small vial."

"Nurse Malone," known as "our queen," is a fine example of a rhyme that honors a member of the nursing staff. In "Soliloquies," Mr. Comstock refers to himself as "a sour-dough drunk," but apparently, he began "to smile in healthy gladness in six months time on Greystone's verdant hill." "That Little Cart of Books," mentions, "Those useless, squandered years of poison booze."

He again, refers to suffering from a lung condition, in "A Sister of Mercy." Note the following stanza,

> "Someway my chest don't hurt so bad
> It seems you drove it off,
> My head is cool and clearer,
> It's not so hard to cough."

A rhyme that gives a glimpse into Mr. Comstock's family, is "The Dreamer," referring to one of his brothers as a "wanderer," the other a "businessman," and finally Mr. Comstock himself, the "dreamer". In "The Comeback," he mentions his membership in the Masonic Brotherhood.

It is apparent from the sad rhyme, "The Fool," Mr. Comstock was married at one time, but lost his wife in childbirth or shortly after, as he tells us,

> "I married and settled down
> With a blue-eyed pal so true,
> O'er the past raised a mighty mound,
> Nor dreamed that the past I'd rue.
>
> So happy, so gloriously glad,
> Were we in our comfy home.
> Nor dreamed we would ever be sad.
> Nor listened to conscience's groan
>
> Complacent I cast away
> All thought of the bygone tools,
> I didn't know I'd have to pay,
> For I was a fool – a fool!
>
> For a babe was given our home.
> And my wife divinely had smiled,
> Then died with heart – rending moan,
> And I started to pay for life's wiles.

For the babe was crippled and blind.
Shapeless as heel-crushed jewel,
The past came back to my mind,
Ah, I was a fool – a fool!"

We feel his empathy and pain, in the poignant rhyme, "Ode to One of Our Little Ones," where he writes a tender tribute, to a "nameless, fatherless" babe, reminding the world not to judge "how legal be his birth, but rather,

"Bear him a merry smile, as wondering there he lies,
He who's destined to hear so little praise;
Bid him be happy and let on the message go
That he is here, and God would have it so."

"One of Life's Tragedies" tells a tale about an unfortunate woman, somewhere in the Far East, named Susan Young. In this rhyme, we get a sense of Mr. Comstock's compassion for women who struggled against addictions and cruel life circumstances, but still managed somehow, to raise their children.

As a native of New Jersey, I particularly appreciate the rhyme, "The Ship of State," dedicated to the "loyal ship New Jersey." New Jersey is often the butt of many jokes, but how many Americans realize the New Jersey Constitution, drafted on July 2, 1776, allowed "all inhabitants of this Colony, of full age, who are worth fifty pounds proclamation money" to vote, "*including non-whites, spinsters, and widows*" (http://www.state.nj.us/nj/about/history/short_history.html). Ironically, both political parties mocked the other for relying on "petticoat electors," referring to women voters, and unfortunately in 1807, this right was restricted to white males. Until that time, however, enlightened New Jersey was at the forefront of both women's and minority rights, including African-American rights. New Jersey legislators were well ahead of their time at the birth of our new Nation, as it took the United States an additional 113 years to grant women the right to vote, by way of the 19th Amendment to the U.S. Constitution, ratified on August 18, 1920, less than 100 years ago (https://www.ourdocuments.gov). African-Americans received the right to vote when the Republicans passed the 15th Amendment to the US Constitution, ratified on February 3, 1870 (http://www.history.com/topics/black-history/voting-rights-act). Mr. Comstock correctly referred to New Jersey, as a "loyal ship."

In "The Hard Riding Kid of Bar T," we read about a young man who wandered in to the Comstock family ranch in Montana, looking for something to eat and was given a job. One day when Mr. Comstock and the young man were riding together, rounding up maverick strays, "The Kid" was bitten by a rattlesnake, while saving Mr. Comstock from falling off a cliff. The Kid's last words, "Tell mother I died like a man," are memorialized in this sad rhyme. Another somber rhyme, "A Tale of Long Ago," relates an experience with his brother "Arch," on an adventure in Alaska in search of gold, when they somehow lost their way on a trail to Fairbanks. Mr. Comstock survived the treacherous journey, but he lost Arch. We can surmise Mr. Comstock was born and raised in Montana, from several rhymes, including, "Memoirs Of The Dawn," where we read one of his best friends was an "Osage Squaw" named, Sleeping Fawn and how she saved his life during a longhorn cattle stampede, by sacrificing her own.

Long before "therapy animals" became the vogue in the mental health community, we learn about Jiggs, in "The Mascot of Greystone Park." "Leaving It Up To You," gives another nod to that venerable profession, occupational therapy, and in his final rhyme, "And Last," Mr. Comstock bids Greystone farewell and shares his plan, to "doctor ailing trees," and mentions his friendship with famed horticulturist and botanist, Luther Burbank,

> "I shall toil 'mongst friendly giants
> Who beckon in the breeze,
> I shall use the verdant knowledge
> Luther Burbank gave to me."

"I'm Telling The World That I'm One," tells us he was admitted to Greystone in August, which is likely August, 1929, because after his release approximately one year later, he started his own horticulture business, *United Landscape Engineers and Foresters,* in Flushing, New York, by July, 1930. He was probably about 35 years of age at the time, because in the rhyme, "Crystal in the Blaze," we read,

INTRODUCTION

"Knowing not I'd be an outcast
Ere I'd aged to thirty-five
That I'd stare from close-barred windows
God! What Fate can do with lives."

The newspaper article, *Renowned Horticulturist, Now Living in Flushing, Relates Experience As Aide to Luther Burbank, Plant Wizard,* The Daily Star, L.I. City (Queens Borough), N.Y., SATURDAY EVENING, July 24, 1930, provides information on Mr. Comstock's life, shortly after his release from Greystone. This article confirms, he "spent the greater part of his life in the wilds of Montana," and worked for "nearly seven years with Luther Burbank, plant wizard." The Daily Star also printed two advertisements for his new business, on July 25 and July 26, 1930, located at "91 Main Street, Flushing, N.Y." Mr. Comstock is listed as "Richard D. Comstock, D.H., General Manager," and promises, "Estimates and Advice Given Free On All Horticultural Services." In the article, he praises the trees of Flushing, as well as provides advice on how to care for, the "372 different varieties of trees on Long Island." He refers to fighting forest fires, as well as his experience laying out the Presidio at Golden Gate Park in San Francisco. Reading further, it is apparent he kept his promise to take his place in the world, "as a producer, not a spoiler," and certainly not a "helpless pest." The article mentions, "he has worked wonders with the flowers and trees on the estates of a number of prominent North Shore residents," and "Mr. Comstock has had a crew of five men working on the famous American elm tree at Northern Boulevard and Whitestone Avenue, Flushing."

In the last paragraph of the article, we learn he was a close friend of the famed Western novelist, Zane Grey. Douglas C. Ingram is also mentioned, as "veteran forest service officer of the West," however, the article mistakenly mentions he was killed in the World War, but as mentioned in "Requiem," Mr. Ingram died fighting the Camas Creek Fire in eastern Washington. It does, however, correctly mention, "The Requiem of the Pines, composed by Mr. Comstock and dedicated to Ingram is one of the best of the poems he has composed and published." Published, thanks to the care provided by the staff of Greystone Hospital, the Print Shop in that old Industrial Building, and the foresight of one *Raver*.

The dedication of the mental health pioneers of the 19th and early 20th centuries, who committed their lives to understanding and treating the mentally ill with dignity and compassion, instead of ridicule and cruelty, must not be taken for granted or forgotten. With the establishment of the Kirkbride hospital system, the once shunned and often abused mentally ill, were given the opportunity to live more fulfilled and productive lives, as well as a chance to recuperate and re-enter society, when possible. It is heartwarming to remember my Dad's service in Greystone's dental clinic, in the old Kirkbride hospital. A first generation American, Dad was born in New York City in 1908, to immigrant parents from Russia and Poland and by the late 1920s, began travelling the country with his banjo to earn money to pay for college. In the early 1930s, he travelled from New Jersey to Mississippi by motorcycle to attend "Ole Miss," the University of Mississippi, graduating in 1934 with a Bachelor of Arts degree.

Dad earned his Doctor of Dental Surgery (DDS) degree at Loyola University in New Orleans in 1938, and shortly after America entered World War II on December 7, 1941, he joined the Army Air Corps at Santa Ana Army Air Base and was commissioned a 1st Lieutenant, on October 31, 1942. One year later, on October 27, 1943, he headed to the Pacific Theatre on the troopship *SS Cape San Juan*, to serve as a dentist for the 855th Aviation Engineer Battalion, and was awarded his "Trusty Shellback" certificate for crossing the equator, on November 6, 1943. Early on the morning of November 11th, the ship was torpedoed by the Japanese submarine, I-21, but thankfully, most survivors were rescued by the combined efforts of American and New Zealand forces, who quickly arrived at the scene.

As so many members of *The Greatest Generation,* Dad was a humble man who rarely discussed his experiences during the war, but thanks to our review of his military records this past Memorial Day, Steve and I discovered his "Shellback" certificate, and could verify he was one of the survivors on the *Cape San Juan,* that fateful day. Shortly after returning from his last active tour of duty with the 4th Medical Battalion, 4th Infantry Division, Frankfurt, Germany in 1959, he continued his career of service at Greystone Park Hospital in 1960, until his death from cancer, in 1972. On a lighter "note," I recently discovered sheet music, titled "The Bombardiers Marching Song," composed by Dad and copyrighted, on June 7, 1943 (*Catalog of Copyright Entries, New Series*, Vol. 38, No. 1, p. 670, 1943).

I wish Dad could have met Mr. Comstock, but he did have the

opportunity to serve alongside the distinguished Reverend Walsh, during his first two years at Greystone. The Reverend Walsh and my Dad, men who dedicated their lives to the service of others without expectation of any special recognition, as is true for all "unsung heroes," should have a little of their stories told, both as an example and an inspiration to future generations. It is apparent from old photos, remaining information about the staff, as well as what Mr. Comstock shares in his *Rhymes,* Greystone was filled with dedicated folks, who spent their lives caring for the helpless and the less fortunate. Throughout the Bible, we read about the importance of helping those who are unable to fend for themselves, including in this verse from the Old Testament,

> "He defended the cause of the poor and needy, and so all went well. Is that not what it means to know me, declares the Lord." (Jeremiah 22:16)

In the New Testament, Jesus states emphatically,

> "Truly I tell you, whatever you did for one of the least of these brothers and sisters of mine, you did for me." (Matthew 25:40)

Our Nation's first hospital was founded in Philadelphia in 1751, by Dr. Thomas Bond and Benjamin Franklin, "to care for the sick-poor and insane who were wandering the streets of Philadelphia" (http://www.uphs. upenn.edu/paharc/features/creation.html). The purpose of the hospital was illustrated by the image of the Good Samaritan and the following inscription,

> "Take care of him and I will repay thee."

From its inception, the "Corporate Vision" of Greystone, and all Kirkbride hospitals, was to defend the cause of the "poor and needy," and care for the "least" or our "brothers and sisters." Mr. Comstock found refuge and treatment for alcoholism in old Greystone Park, six years before Alcoholics Anonymous was founded, in 1935 (http://www.aa.org). He also received "state of the art" treatment for his damaged lungs and for the "Posttraumatic Stress Disorder" (PTSD), he most likely also suffered, over

50 years before the American Psychiatric Association acknowledged PTSD as a diagnosable disorder, in 1980 (https://www.ptsd.va.gov). When we think of the old campus of Greystone Park Hospital, we should not only remember the deteriorated condition of the once magnificent 19th century Kirkbride buildings and facilities, stories of patient overcrowding, neglect and abuse, and the unfortunate experimentation with horrific "therapies," before the introduction of psychoactive drugs, but also remember the dedicated and compassionate staff and their noble efforts to make the lives of the suffering and the helpless, many abandoned by family and friends, more tolerable, pleasant, and productive.

Finally, let us also remember "Kirkbride" Greystone, as a *Monarch of Mansions,* as we read in the rhyme, "Thanks to Commissioner Ellis." William J. Ellis was commissioner of the Department of Institutions & Agencies, established in New Jersey in 1919, to oversee the state's programs relating to psychiatric and medical care, correctional institutions, and the guardianship of children (http://www.nj.gov/state/archives). At the beginning of *Rhymes,* in "Preface in Rhyme," Mr. Comstock refers to Greystone, as "this refuge mercy-marked that's known to you as Greystone Park." He goes on to say,

> "Could you who read this book but know
>   The good that from this hilltop flows,
> If you could see the joy gained
>   By mortals who have known but pain,"

The rhyme continues for several pages and ends with thanks, "For reading rhymes of my poor pen," and hoping "you'll sometimes think of me, as Friend Eternal, R.D.C." On the final page of *Rhymes*, in "My Sojourn at Greystone," R.D.C. leaves us with no doubt that his sojourn of healing, did indeed end on the joyous note of a life renewed,

> "And as the butterfly emanates from the cocoon I have emerged from the shell of darkness and sordidness and stand looking out into a joyous world of normalcy and achievement."

You are thought of gratefully, *Friend Eternal, R.D.C.*

The Man Of God

He came while the presses whirred,

    Came with a brotherly smile,

Brought a message of kindly words,

    And tarried to chat awhile.

Came to purchase my book of rhymes,

    His speech with a friendly nod

Told me plain my book would win,

    For he was a man of God.

He didn't stay so very long,

    But he left a something there

That made a sob change to a song,

    And peace seemed in the air,

Some folks saw but a kindly man,

    But I who 'mongst trees have trod

So long, could clearly understand

    That he was a man of God.

So like a shady, spready oak

    His spirit sent its wave

To welcome babies, 'ere they'd spoke,

    And restful make the grave.

Yes, like a towering western pine

    His strength swept o'er the sod

Like redwood smiling calm at time,

    So stood this man of God.

Before you, Reverend Walsh, there plays

    A groping world that needs you so,

Where wearied souls have lost their way,

    And know not where to stay or go.

The twisted, tinseled path of sin,

    Like me, they long have trod.

Now that they mourn, "It might have

        been,"

    Please help them, man of God.

Pour o'er their troubled, restless souls

    The balm you granted me,

Paint on their hearts' still vacant scrolls

    The scene "Eternity."

You are the first to buy my book,

    Wherein I've sowed the seed

That I do so much want to brook

Some other sinner's need.

And to me it's a glorious sign

That rhymes of us who plod

On dreary road send first their lines

To sincere man of God.

Author's Note:

The above rhyme was inspired by Rev. Joseph E. Walsh when he called at the Print Shop to order one of the books.

His general manner was naturally friendly and he spoke of some of my past writings with such appreciation, that I considered it a good omen that a minister of the Gospel be the first to purchase my book, and crude as it's wording be it means much to me.

REQUIEM OF THE PINES

It got you, Doug, like you said it would,

    You died 'midst the smoke and pine tree flame.

As noble as any trunk you stood,

    As clean as an oak, and just as game,

It got you, Doug, but your spirit's here,

    As we grab our clothes and the tools and run,

When the Chief's curt orders ring out clear:

    "Check her, boys, or the west strip's done."

And as we swing to the water tanks

    We breathe your name as we dash on through

The outer blaze of the Red Fiend's flanks,

    We fight hot hell like you used to do.

It got you Doug, but pard of mine,

    Whom I've seen laugh 'midst the curling flames,

You've done your best for our lordly pines,

    And man, oh! man, you blinked out game.

REQUIEM OF THE PINES

Yes, it got you, pard, but I know you're there

    Just above the flames as we spread our lines,

As we pull cross-cuts with half-cursed prayers

    And bleed for the lives of our lofty pines.

Remember that siege in Oregon,

    When we'd fought three days on the main ridge strip,

When we swung our lads at the streak of dawn,

    Me blind and you with a busted hip.

When crew after crew had to quit and run,

    And you were the very last man to go.

You gasped out, "Dick, I guess I'm done,"

    But God and the bull pines murmured, "No."

But the Red Death finally brought you down,

    And a hero passed from the choking smoke

To a great reward where there are no clowns

    Who blow a blaze into ghastly joke.

With a heart still young, tho' I sort of wheeze

    -Rememher my lungs got seared at Paine's-

I still plug on at saving trees,

    Following trails of the big-tree game.

But it won't be long till I join you, "Doug,"

    And we'll climb the peak to the look-out's shack,

Where we'll guard our trees 'gainst the blood-red thug,

And clear a way for the rangers' tracks.

Sleep on, oh! Doug, in your western grave,

We'll carry on as you'd want us to.

The spruce and the fir and the pines you saved

Shall stand· as a monument to you.

Author's Note:

In memoriam to my friend of many years, Douglas C. Ingram, long a member of that gallant and very often heroic body of men who constitute the rangers and employees of the United States Forestry Service, whose tremendous importance the. entire country realizes more and more.

Douglas Ingram was an officer of the Service and gave his life in defense of the forests he loved. Side by side we have fought and suffered, hungered and sleepless, striving to subdue flames of sorrow end devastation.

To clean. fearless, patient, big-hearted, rugged "Doug," the "Friend of the Forests," as the then Secretary of the Interior, Franklin K. Lane called him, do I dedicate this rhyming chronicle with the silent salutation that only those who have been seared and blistered fighting the scourge of the tall timber can appreciate.

Offered to the world with the sincere respect of one who knows the trees, — and loves them.

Preface In Rhyme

You folks out in the busy world,

    Who laugh and sigh and brave life's churl,

Who laugh and mourn and grieve and sing,

    Whose heart and hand have everything

That goes to make up human strife,

    That fills the catalog of life,

You who read my jumbled rhymes,

    Who see where they are blurred sometimes,

Just pass the blurs they're only tears

    Shed by us who face the years

Behind the silent, towering walls

    Where humans answer human calls

As best they can, and we are spared

    All pain, for doctor's knowledge shares

Its wondrous work with gentle nurse,

    Who from the shadows take the curse,

And draw the sting of shortening breath,

 When at the last we robe for death.

And 'twixt my rambling, uncouth lines,

 If you read grief, don't think we pine

For lack of treatment, help or care,

 For those three things are everywhere

About this refuge mercy-marked

 That's known to you as Greystone Park.

Could you who read this book but know

 The good that from this hilltop flows,

If you could see the joy regained

 By mortals who have known but pain,

If you could see the things we see,

 Your very heart would sing with glee,

But still there are some gathered here,

 Who'll always dwell in manse of fear,

Who never can cast off their train

 Griefs that curse a sickened brain.

We stumble on through cheerless· years,

 With pain and sorrow, trials and fears.

It's hard to bear, but well we know

 'Tis just and God would have it so,

And if some one of you have kin

PREFACE IN RHYME

Or kith, or friends, these walls within,

I'd like to speak a word for them,

For maybe they don't swing a pen,

As I so love to ever do.

But they're content, I swear to you,

For I have watched them as they walked,

Played, and worked, and laughed, and talked.

My friends, I swear to each of you

There're many happy whole years thru'.

For comfort here is surely claimed,

And every type of merry game,

With Occupation's golden seams

Are spreading out in greater beams,

And blessing those who would forget

The bygone years with past regrets.

So if my rhymes don't make you glad,

I'm sorry, but I'm not so sad.

I've just resigned myself to ·Fate.

And now my life tale I relate,

To warn some other wandering one

Before his youthful years be done,

That he can note my pain-blazed trails,

And steer away from haunting wails,

Perhaps some fellow man may lose

    By my drear rhymes his craze for booze.

If one drink on like me they'll fall

    And wake betwixt the sullen walls,

With body shaken, mind a mess,

    An outcast wreck, a helpless pest.

And others who shall read my rhymes,

    When sickness first attacks their minds

May go before the illness grows

    To psychiatrists who always know

Just what to do for weary minds,

    To help them leave their grief behind.

So would I send these jumbled rhymes

    Out where my friends and foes in line

Can read and maybe just forget,

    For an hour or so their dire regrets,

I hope that all of you will read

    And like the verses, may they feed

Some hungry heart that often pines

    In lonely grief like that of mine.

And if some downcast one be brought

    A glimpse of sunshine from my thoughts,

Then, folks, I'd sure be mighty glad

PREFACE IN RHYME

If I have cheered one who was sad.

You know, folks, as I write these lines,

    It seems you're all old friends of mine.

I've written each month just for you,

    It's thrilled my heart to do it, too.

And, friends, behind these rusty bars,

    I've stared up at the jolly stars,

And nigh to tears thanked Him up there,

    That I could write my simple wares

In manner that you liked to read.

    To me it was a golden seed

That's grown and blossomed out into

    A shady oak where birds fly through,

And build their feathery, comfy nests,

    And send their songs from joyous breasts,

Where aged folks who peacefully wait

    Their call to those great pearly gates

May sit down in the cooling shade,

    And dream about the older glades.

Where kiddies stretch out in the grass,

    And count the sheep and lambs that pass.

So, folks, I'll thank you once again

    For reading rhymes of my poor pen.

So now I'll seal this rhyming book

    And melt back into shadowed nook

To wistful gaze out thru' the bars

    At dancing Venus, bold, bright Mars.

And hope you'll get an hour's relief

    By turning thru' unvarnished leaves

That have fallen about me o'er the hill

    Where Greystone Park sends out its will.

And· hope you'll sometimes think of me, As

    friend eternal,   R. D. C.

THE GIRL FROM HOME

We were hittin' for Khartoum, me an' Peg Leg Billy Dunn,

  We had caught a horseboat charted for the Rajah of Shakun,

An' Peg Leg had a fever, not a docior on the boat,

  With me a-boilin' water an' tryin' to cool his throat.

We was headin' for Bwango an' we didn't lose no time,

  'Cause we yearned to see the boomin' of the K. B. diamond

    mines.

Peg Leg kept on gettin' sicker, an' when the floatin' scow

  Churned in to Abbol-Dharbo and stopped her muddy prow,

I had some coolies help me carry Peg Leg to the town,

  Where there wasn't any doctor nor a white man to be found.

But I bought a wild cane tarri and made Bill a mossy bed,

  And then I hit the village for some kind of Dago red.

I got the liquor, fixed up Peg a breath-destroying swig,

  Then bargained for some corn meal and a quarter cut of pig.

I hired a wrinkled grandma to do her best for Bill,

An' she cooked some roots an' berries an' made him drink his fill.

But he kept on gettin' sicker an' he raved on thro' the night

    Of his old home in New Jersey, till the break of morning's light.

Soon I got to feelin' dizzy an' a tightness at my throat,

    An' Peg began to cuss me for not takin' to the boat.

He wanted me to catch the scow while I could get away,

    To leave while I had yet a chance, but hell, I had to stay.

I couldn't leave a buddy in that ·God-forsaken land

    Where the flies are big as hornets and mosquitos big as hams,

So I cussed him out and stretched beneath the shadow of the shack,

    While Peg raved about New Jersey.an' 'lowed he was goin' back.

When night came down I sure was a plenty sick, I'll say,

    And tossed an' sweat till mornin' while Peg just fought an' raved.

An' then one mornin' when the sun seemed sort of bloody red,

    When a hundred million needles were a-jabbin' thru' my head,

I thot I saw a vision, a mirage; loud I cursed

    When it didn't leave, I rubbed my eyes. My God, it was a nurse!

Well I blinked out of the picture an' that little Jersey girl

    Took right hold and went to doping, talk about your priceless

        pearls.

When I came to in the morning she was watchin' by the fire,

    With her gentle eyes wide open, but lookin' mighty tired.

I was sick but Peg was sicker, an' I told her about him,

    An' the sweetheart back in Jersey an' her eyes got sort o' dim,

As she patted soft my shoulder an' whispered 'neath her breath,

"You've been faithful to your buddy, faithful even unto death."

An' she pointed where pore Peg was stretched, a shawl across his

face.

An' I saw her lips a-movin' in a prayer of hallowed grace.

She helped a native dig a grave, an' laid old Peg away,

As the blazing disk of fire sank in bluish crimson waves.

An' one night when I was stronger we talked beside the shack,

An' I asked her where she come from, when she meant to hit

it back.

Then she turned an' gazed out at the grave amongst the jungle's vines

And a flood of saddened misery from her eyes burst into mine.

She didn't cry—a nervy lass—-but her shoulders trembled some.

She said, "I'm from New Jersey. For Billy I had come.

We were planning to be married when Bill quit roving round.

He had promised me to quit his trails and that he'd settle down.

But I was lonely, wearied, and had some money saved,

At last I found my darling, 'twas to lay him in his grave."

Well, we took the boat back up the Nile and a steamer for the

States.

She went back to her nursing, an' I still tempted Fate

By traveling, sailing, rambling, but I'll ne'er forget that nurse

Who buried poor old Peg Leg Dunn in land by God accursed.

NOBODY'S SWEETHEART

It is so strange, I'm all alone,

    No sweetheart at my side,

All that I touch seems cold as stone,

    And memories deride.

I've slipped on dangerous, darkened ice,

    And sorrow's o'er my brow.

I can but pay the crimson price,

    I'm nobody's sweetheart now.

I've lost them all, those jolly pals,

    For whom I cared so much,

Now I am numbered with the "gals,"

    'Whom no good man will touch.

I gave my lips to please their will.

    I opened wide my heart,

And now I'm cast aside as nil,

    Erased from friendly chart.

Just one of the simple, weaker kind,

    Who just keep on somehow,

Believing love is only blind.

    But I'm nobody's sweetheart now.

I've always worked and earned my way

    By sincere, honest toil.

Oh, why should I now have to pay,

    Because my life is soiled?

The mother's sons who swore their love,

    Then mocked at marriage vows,

Walk on past me, their eyes above,

    And I'm nobody's sweetheart now.

I guess I'm awful, awful bad,

    That's what most good folks say,

As they scorn me, alone and sad,

    Out of their social rays.

So here's to death in this small vial,

    I've done wrong I'll allow,

But I'm going to leave this vale of trials,

    'Cause nobody wants me now.

THE GUTTER TAKES BACK ITS OWN

I hailed me a maiden from the slums,

    In her rags, and her ignorant drawl.

I fitted her out with the best that comes,

    In clothing, hat, shoes, and all.

Sent her to high-toned boarding school

    To learn what life can be,

To learn to breast life's cultured pools

    And see what learned ones see.

She came on back when her terms were thru',

    But she fled to the old life's foam,

'Mongst the dazzling lights she downward flew,

    And the gutter took back its own.

I pulled a bearded youth from the reek

    Of a ten-cent lodging den,

Dressed him up to help him seek

THE GUTTER TAKES BACK ITS OWN

A place in the ranks of men.

I made him a job in my mining camp,

And let him pay off the crew,

Tore from his face the look of a tramp,

And he seemed to be coming through.

But one sad day I felt the knife

Of pain, for the lad had flown

With some yellow coin to the other life,

And the gutter took back its own.

But I hailed yet another red light girl,

Gave her a home and rest.

She shook the old, degrading whirl,

And tried to attain the best.

I took her to church and her voice rang clear

And sweet ·as a thrush's song,

She sent her song that the world might hear

That right had won over wrong.

She married a lad with a noble aim,

And to-day her kiddies three

Always rush from their childish games

To toddle around with me.

She paid for her sister of the night,

Who sank back in the scum

Called by the white way's blinding light,

But the gutter got only one.

So I picked another man from the line,

Drunken, and dirty, and mean.

I took him out 'mongst the western pines,

And gave him a four-horse team.

He didn't know a horse from a goat,

But before the summer was done

I knew no booze would burn his throat

For I, not the gutter, had won,

To-day he's king of his own wide lands,

A wife, and a happy home,

But Fate has tricks in her fickle hands,

For she made me the gutter's own.

I JUST NOTICED

She was a little nervous, grayhaired old lady

With an old fashioned, jerky round hat with

A couple of faded old gold-cloth flowers on

One side, and a big bow of velvet on the other,

Which was loose and threatened every minute

To blow away in the wind.

She had walked up the hill from the Reception

Building and was a little out of breath and

Flustered, and as she watched the string of cars,

For the time being in endless stream at the

Crossing place, she kept darting worried,

Bird-like glances this way and that, as she

Waited on the curb for the traffic to change,

All the time clutching the precious packages

Which you just know contained big brown

Ginger cookies or doughnuts or coffee cake

With apple jelly, and her black, old fashioned

Skirt looked old and rusted like and had been

Carefully patched several places and it

Came right down to her flat-heeled, dollar

Ninety-eight cent shoes with the heels run

Down, and the toes scuffed. Anyway, she

Wanted to get across to the Main Building

And it was just one o'clock when visiting

Hours begin, when just as the officer

Stopped the traffic to let her go across,

I saw a tall, carefully dressed man who looked

Very modern, step out of a shiny car that

Cost three thousand dollars, and who had a

Large diamond ring, and an expensive gold

Watch chain, and an imported Japanese muffler,

And ten dollar cordevan gloves, take off his

Hat right out there in the rain and sleet,

And walk right up to the little old bird-like

Lady with the packages, and the dumpy

Hat, and old shoes and everything, and take

Her packages and her big pocket book and

Then take hold of her arm mighty careful

Like and looking to each side in a very careful

40

I JUST NOTICED

Manner he guided her across the street,

And the little old lady bobbed her head and

With an out-of-date curtesy thanked him

Again and again, before she climbed the

Steps up to the usher, for her pass to

Visit a husband who had made Greystone Park

His home for twenty years.

And after she had turned to leave him, the

Fine looking modern dressed man with the big

Diamond on his finger, and the expensive

Watch chain, and the imported Japanese

Scarf, stood there just gazing, gazing, a

Far away look in his eyes, until the little

Old lady in the little dinky hat had bobbed

Out of sight, and he seemed to be thinking

About something pleasant and gentle, for he

Smiled just a little, and held the band

That had held her packages and her pocket

Book to his nose, to see if he could find

The odor of old roses and lavender, and he did,

And he stepped thoughtfully into the big shiny

Car, and drove away, and I scratched my leg with

The toe of my other foot, and

Went on back to my office in the Print Shop.

And I guess I've scribbled enough, and besides

I smell beans and cabbage cookin' so it's me

For the ward pronto and

That's all.

Nurse Malone

Authors Note:

In this poem, I but voice the unspoken thoughts of thousands of patients to whom Miss Molly Malone has been ever bulwark against trouble and pain.

Noting her unselfish interest in the patients has granted me one of the most profound inspirations of my life.

When we're deep in silent sorrow,

    And some trouble gnaws our feelings,

When we think how nice 'twould be if we could die,

    There's a friend today, tomorrow,

Who slaps our griefs a-reeling,

    Who doesn't ask a foolish how or why.

She is quiet, and yet she's speedy

    When a patient sends a summons

For medicine, or food, or anything

    That is needed by the needy,

You can see her smile a-coming,

    And you bet your specs it gets there on the wing.

She just knows when things ain't breaking

    Like they ought to be, and aids you

When you're muttering 'twixt a curse and prayer,

    While your tortured soul is aching,

She sends a smile that fades you,

    And soon you're free of misery and despair.

With her honest eyes a-gleaming.

    And ·her Irish voice resounding

With the pity of the Virgin at the Cross,

    With her tranquil face a-beaming,

And her faithful heart a-pounding,

    With sympathy for ill ones sorrow tossed.

Who is this that we are lauding,

    We the patients who·have suffered,

And granted peace with her upon the throne?

    She's our Queen, and we're applauding,

'Cause she's always been· our buffer.

    Tell the cockeyed world we're cheering

      Nurse Malone.

SALUTATION TO A
BRAVE SPIRIT

Ah, gladsome maiden who once used to gaily dance,

Fantastic whirling, leaping, flitting at your play,

You who pleased great masses when with smiling glance,

You danced so merrily and drove dull care away.

But now your once bright smile is oh, so sad,

Because no more you flaunt your lilting fairy race

Before the crowds, who so enjoyed thy stepping glad,

Do you think we forget thy tripping, blithesome grace?

No, little sister, who must now walk steady, slow,

We'll ne'er forget your trouble-chasing dance,

Our hearts are with you, girl, no matter where you go,

Thy dance still lives its memory by time enhanced,

Truly thou art one real sportsman from the heart,

For never hast thou of thy sorrow whined,

And ah, so few knew of the aching. quivering dart

That lay within that guiltless soul of thine.

Weep not, oh sorrowed heart. but trail thy way along;

So young art thou, and fair thy glowing face.

For you have cheered so many by thy terpsichorean songs

And thou hast only started in life's oft gyrating race.

And you, oh grieving girl, have here made many friends

Who hold you high in admiration and esteem,

Who trust and hope that fickle fate will yet expend

A change for you, interpreter of Peter Pan's bright dreams.

And at the great, long rest when God inscribes your name

Upon his favorite's page, in that Eucheristic book,

He'll write, "Here's one brave heart who lost a treasured game,

Yet weakened not when trouble her sole glory took."

SOLILOQUIES

There are lives that dwell in darkness,

    In a dank, beshadowed canyon,

Where there's mighty little light creeps in at most.

    There they rot in sullen starkness,

Like a coroner-sentenced mankin,

    Their existence as important as a post.

They deserve a world of pity,

    For the mold that was cast for them,

There are some who have inherited their ills,

    And their life's a tuneless ditty.

Sad, depressive hours that gore them,

    Till at last some of them come here· on the hill.

But there're thousands that are reeling,

    Out in that world of mortals

That are growing sicker, weaker every day,

    Who have turned deaf ears to pealing

Of the bells of knowledge's portals,

　　And before they die the fiddler shall be paid.

When you sink in drear depression.

　　And your nerves are taut and straining,

When you sit and stare and mumble, "What's the use?"

　　Give your doctor clear expression

Of your illness; you'll be gaining

　　Time that you'll regret the losing like the deuce.

Lay your cards down on the table,

　　Tell the psychiatrist your trouble,

Keep no secret from his calculating eye.

　　He will help you, for he's able,

With the case of blowing bubbles,

　　If you'll work with him and answer *hows* and *whys*.

You may think the world's against you,

　　That your life is simply wasted,

You may swear you haven't got an earthly friend,

　　Though it seems that grief has fenced you,

There are joys you've never tasted,

　　And you've many years of mirth before the end.

So for sake of years of pleasure,

　　Read yourself, and if you're shaking

With some nervousness that keeps you in the ruts,

SOLILOQUIES

Take your own mind's careful measure

Before it starts to breaking,

Don't go crazy when all you need is guts.

Tell the mental "doc" your failings,

Even if it sets you blushing,

You won't faze the "doc" with ghost-in-closet tale;

Let him know where you are ailing,

And do doggone little hushing,

From the wild and racy past tear down the veil.

For these mental hygiene croakers

Know their stuff, I tell you, buddy,

For they've snapped me from a hectored living death,

They held deuces wild with jokers

That made me sit and study,

And they taught me how to breathe a healthy breath.

They have stripped from me the madness

That disease had sown and cultured,

They have granted me the spirit and the will

To smile in healthy gladness,

When I'd once frowned like a vulture,

In six months time on Greystone's verdant hill.

Oh, I'm just a burly rambler

Who has been unusual lucky,

In garnering quite a pile of filthy gold.

    I've been just an aimless gambler,

With a trail of booze that's mucky,

    And the doctors snapped me up ere I was old.

Now I'd like to pass the favor

    On down the line to others,

And so within my funny metred rhymes

    I try to let my neighbors

Know about a grateful brother

    Whose whole darn life had not been worth a dime.

Till with Greystone's mighty system

    I was cleansed and taught and treated;

God! how those doctors can untangle minds.

    They take crooked brains and twist 'em,

They cool thought that's overheated,

    And they taught a sour-dough drunk to fashion rhymes.

There was mighty Marcus Curry—

    New Jersey's need had stormed him,

And Drs. Laatsch, Gebertig, Palmer, Washburn too.

    There was good old "Doc" McMurray—

God lost the mould that made him.

    Each one of these fine chaps helped pull me through,

So you poor floor-walking creatures,

SOLILOQUIES

Why have touch of dread psychosis

Don't delay; get to a clinic somewhere now.

They will change your brooding features,

When they get your diagnosis,

And you'll find that you have learned to laugh somehow.

THE PORTRAIT

Author's Note:

In the following rhyme I attempt to picture the success and wondrous benefit that has been and is being granted to humanity through the efforts of Dr. G.B. McMurray, Senior resident Physician at the New Jersey Hospital for Nervous and Mental Diseases at Greystone Park.

Tireless, unselfish, understanding and sympathizing with worries and cares of the patient he has carved for himself a noble design in the hearts of many, and most of all to us who strive to attain a state of normalcy.

Come, artist of exalted world-wide name,

    And bring with you your brush and paint of gold;

A portrait you must paint, and call it "Life of Fame,"

    A picture that to some will ne'er grow old.

I wish it spread across yon lofty, spray-dashed clift

    Beneath which winds the road of mortal man,

That all who pass need but their eyes to lift,

    To view the face of him who guards his clan.

No gaudy ribboned medals on his breast,

    No memories of a mass of tortured foes,

THE PORTRAIT

No *Croix de Guerre* for fighting on his chest,

    With medals seen by God alone, he goes.

Paint me a countenance firm and free of guile,

    A high forehead and that's squared and free,

With steady, kindly eyes that cloak a smile

    And hold a promise sworn, of great sincerity.

Draw finely on thy art, thy greatest skill

    Must make this picture true, for all the land

Shall know the strength, the wisdom of his will.

    Carve fine the features, so that e'en a child will understand.

Listen close, magician of inspired brush,

    Miss not one word of what I have to say,

For I must hurry on into the silent hush

    Of death, and this great picture needs must stay.

Must stand there on that rearing cliff of stone,

    That suffering ones, whom he has granted aid,

Keep on the well-beat path which he has shown,

    That they may stronger be, nor feel afraid.

As you would struggle with the sacred joy

    Reflected by the sunset's mellowed grace,

The wave of pure beauty unalloyed

    Upon a little child's angelic face

As you would strive to catch the e'er endearing look

Of loving wife who bids her mate a last farewell,

As you would toil to catch the prayer by sorrow shook,

On this I bid you toil and tell my story well.

Spread me that sincere, faithful knowing look

Out o'er that rugged rock-bound wall.

Where it shall stand, tho' storm assailed and earthquake shook,

Up 'mongst the clouds, cleansed by the rain drops' fall.

Ten thousand years must this great picture stand,

For ages it shall shine o'er land and lea,

A symbol for the ill ones of the land,

A light-house for the helpless ones at sea.

Oh, had I but an omnipotent mind,

Could I but write the things I feel and see,

The tongue of Homer so that this one rhyme

Might, with the picture, stand eternally,

But I am just a trembling, fearful one,

Who cowers in the shadows and the gloom

To wait until this strange, wierd farce be done,

Who, cringing, waits the tocsin's peal of doom.

See, painter, in the door on down the hall,

Now shaking hands with that demented soul,

There stands your model 'gainst the darkened wall;

'Tis he whose countenance goes on the scroll.

THE PORTRAIT

Quick, catch now that pitying look upon his face

    As he speaks low with understanding tone,

Catch that quiet smile which, blended with God's grace,

    Sweeps out and clears away the madman's groans.

That is the look I'd have on yon great mountain's brow

    Up where the lightning's flash and thunder's roll

Light up his face and tell all humans how

    He smiled while giving up his life for sickened souls.

Link not my name with this great work of art;

    I seek but rest, while he has won bis fame.

Mine but the whim of wearied, grateful heart,

    One of the thousands of his mentally lame.

And now, away, and paint this portrait o'er the sea,

    While I sink back into the shadowed haunting walls,

Where I await the beckon of Dame Fate to me,

    Until God lets me leave this sordid, useless all.

KNIGHT OF THE
JANGLING KEYS

When the silence of night screams the loudest

    And regret sweeps in like a tide,

When remorse brings the sight of lost treasures

    Gaunt ghosts lurking close at your side.

A welcome sound breaks the silence,

    And someway you feel more at ease,

As Meredith swings down the hall-way

    With a handfull of jangling keys.

Straight from the shoulder his bearing,

    Square as a cornice is square,

Erect, his head meets the masses,

    In his eyes burns sincerity's flare.

KNIGHT OF THE JANGLING KEYS

Watching and striving for ill ones

    Serving at duties' knees,

Noting all signs of a fever,

    This Knight of the Jangling Keys.

Somehow there's a song in their jangling

    As merrily they twinkle and chime,

And you know by rounds of the hour

    It helps you to pass by the time.

For when you are nervous and worried

    And the shadow frown awful at you,

You long for the sound of a human,

    And any old racket will do.

You get from those keys lots o' pleasure,

    Somehow you can rest more at ease

When Joe makes his rounds thru the darkness.

    The Knight of the Jangling Keys.

And sometimes if you get the toothache

    Or a pain in your tummy somewhere,

He'll hustle and call for a doctor

    You'll get help if Joe knows your cares.

He asks for no thanks nor plaudits,

    He is glad if a soul he can please,

And he's cheered many hearts that were burdened,

This Knight of the Jangling Keys.

There's many a lad on the North-side,

　　Found rest when they waited in pain,

Till the clanking keys told them plainly

　　That he'd started his ward-rounds again.

Doing his bit for the ill ones,

　　To aid them through smiting disease,

Watchful his guard through the starkness.

　　This Knight of the Jangling Keys.

THAT LITTLE CART OF BOOKS

There are times when hours drag and lag so tiresome

 And you cannot seem to find a thing to do,

When everything is wrong and seems to roil you,

 The whole big world and all that's in it blue.

When your fellow creatures sit in silent brooding

 And everywhere you get a dull grave look,

As you thumb some dog-eared magazine of fiction

 While you're waiting for that little cart of books.

When a drizzly rain is beating 'gainst the window

 And in your knees you feel the rheumatiz,

When you cannot find the way out of your jungle,

 As you face the past and find no friendly phiz,

There's only one thing that can make you happy.

 As carefree as a duckling in a brook.

It's the coming of the girl who brings to greet you

 That little two-wheeled cart, chock full of books.

To us birds who've tramped and sailed along the Congo

    Midst desert's heat, or ghostly blinding snows,

Across Sahara, or mi9st Klondyke's freezing

    On a trail that's ending where God only knows.

When we're locked up 'mongst a lot of wearied sick ones

    And we long to take a hike with line and hooks,

You can bet your false teeth, mister, it's a blessing

    When that girl wheels in that little cart of books.

I was sitting in the reading room this morning

    And I was feeling rather dull and blue,

Pattering drops were tapping 'gainst the window

    It seemed as tho the sun could not break thru.

As the hours seemed to pause, my heart grew lonely,

    I tried to think about some canyon's nook,

While I wondered when I'd get some more "forgetters"

    That were carried in that little cart of books.

The past and all its folly seemed to hector.

    A glorious future I had tossed away,

Age creeping on and grinning close behind me

    A mocking ghost that seemed to swing and sway.

It wasn't very pleasant to my vision:

    Those useless, squandered years of poison booze,

For I'd tossed a game with death at many sittings

And hoped that I would be the one to lose.

When fame I scorned and great career forsook.

Now on a claim staked out for those demented,

Just longing for a little cart of books.

For books that grip you, wipe away the misery

And bring a smile to heart by sorrow shook.

You can swim the rapids, scale the peaks of mountains,

When the girl brings in that little can of books.

And now the clouds are gone, and sunlight's gleaming,

Me with a book that's brought me o'er the seas.

Gone is the gloom and peacefully I'm reading

About the kind of man I used to be.

God bless you, friendly pal, who brings our manna,

You've cheered up men that grief had cruelly hooked.

Roll down the sands of time, at manse and hovel

There're those who wait to glimpse your cart of books.

Author's Note:

This rhyme is dedicated to the library workers of the world.

I wish that you who donate books and reading to our library might share the pleasure and relaxation that we derive from them.

To see our librarian with her little cart of books is, to many many patients, a sight of joy and cheerful anticipation.

Arm in arm with Occupational Therapy, library work, which eases the troubled mind even tho the troubles be imaginary, is fast becoming recognized as an important factor in the treatment of nervous and mental diseases.

THE SYMPHONY

A bunch of the patients were shaking a hoof

    On North-Two-One one night;

The dominie sat on the player's stool,

    And was playing "Lead Kindly Light."

When down the hall from the section wards

    There stumbled a weird looking man,

With eyes like a leapord, furious red,

    And a foolish look on his pan.

I got to wondering who he was

    And from which ward he came;

His lanky form was clothed in jeans,

    And he walked just a little lame.

There're men that somehow hold your eyes,

    Tho' you can't tell how nor why,

But they make yo'u think of an old blind dog,

    Who has wandered away to die.

THE SYMPHONY

Well, this bird gripped hard upon your mind,

    As he shuffled up to a chair,

With apology peeping from worried eyes,

    In a sort of a helpless stare.

Then the dominie wearied of picking tunes

    So he left the piano stool.

Then the stranger climbed from his easy chair

    And flopped down there like a fool.

For a moment he paused, and a chill wind swept

    O'er our hearts; and our souls were swayed,

As the stranger fondled the keys, that wept

    Of love and the better days.

So soft they rang each throbbing note:

    'Twas a treat for an angel's ear.

Tho' plain you saw by the patient's face

    That the notes were full of tears.

A plea for one who'd left him flat;

    A call to a deathless love;

A prayer for one who had tossed his heart

    To crash from the heights above.

You felt like you wanted to help him plead

    With the mate who had tossed aside:

God! What a look on a creature's face

As the music swept it's tide.

The music twinkled and seemed to trill

    With the joy of a fond wife's voice.

It fairly swept you o'er sylvan hills,

    Till your very soul rejoiced.

You felt a curl against your cheek,

    Saw a pair of smiling eyes:

In her presence you felt unworthy, meek,

    Like a sinner in Paradise.

You shut your eyes, and felt the kiss

    Of a being beyond all worth;

You felt the clasp of a baby's hand

    And you wanted to shout in mirth.

You lived the days of your honeymoon,

    With your own pal at your side.

Is that a smile on the patient's face

    As he boasts of his wonderful bride?

Then the music sank with a chilling moan,

    So low that 'twas harely drawn,

But you grieved from a heart that was stark with fear,

    Of a love that had died and gone.

You sobbed at the side of an empty crib,

    You hugged one little red shoe,

THE SYMPHONY

You stared at a hastily written note

    That a woman had left for you.

You groped with a mind that had lost its trend

    Of a soul, alone in the dark,

Then the music crashed with a mighty twang—

    And the end at Greystone Park.

The attendants came and led him away

    Back to ward Two-Two,

Who he was or where he is from

    Not one of us ever knew.

But after we had straightened up the chairs,

    When the songs for the night were through,

Down close to the piano's bright pedals

    Was a baby's worn red shoe.

Author's Note:

Dedicated to Mrs. Margaret Farrell, depicting her attitude towards all patients.

A Sister Of Mercy

Thanks, nurse, that's so much better,

    I'm easier, I declare.

Before you came I thought I'd die,

    And that's the truth, I swear.

Thanks for that nice hot cocoa,

    Gee, nurse, 'twas awful good!

How did you come to think of me?

    So very few folks would.

Say, nurse your eyes are just as kind

    As tender true and glad

As my gentle little mother,

    The only friend I've had.

Someway my chest don't hurt so bad

    It seems you drove it off,

My head is cool and clearer,

    It's not so hard to cough.

A SISTER OF MERCY

Before you came in Nursie

    I was staring at the wall

And wondering if I really wished

    To live this life of gall.

No one to give a darn for me,

    No one to understand

No wife to wait at home for me,

    No kiddie's waving hand.

Just homely, bearded, awkward,

    With a heart still beating bold.

Wearied' out-cast, sickened,

    Alone —and growing old

Just waiting for the Range-boss

    To tell me when to ride

Through purple-curtained canyon,

    Where buddie's spirits glide.

I've dealt strange hands from dog-eared decks,

    But the cards were always square,

I've played the game with deuces wild,

    And grinned at loser's share

But you have been so good to me,

    It makes me clear forget

That but today I longed to die,

Those thoughts I now regret.

"Won't you drop in once more, Nursie,

    Before your shift is through?

You sure have perked me up a lot,

    And I'm much obliged to you."

Now I'm up and well again,

    They've taken the nurse away.

She's been sent to the Clinic,

    To cheer other sick one's days.

Where e'er she goes, what e'er she does,

    May our Savior keep her free

From harm, for like an angel

    She administered to me.

That Chap They Call McNuff

I could tell you many a story

 Of the chap this rhyme salutes,

I could tell of the light and glory

 That he brought to lives once mute.

On duty as charge attendant

 In the realm of our famed C. B.

With deeds of worth resplendent

 Which shall live eternally.

Friend to the wearied repining,

 A slave in the hour of need,

Panacea with restful lining,

 He harks to a plea and heeds.

There's many a patient been granted

 Health when sickness was rife,

When their lifeline downward slanted

And death held aloft its knife.

I have talked with those be has aided,

    And from them learned more than enough

To inspire a pen more jaded

    Of this chap they call McNuff.

He has wrestled with stiffened muscles,

    He has toiled with the blind G. P.

He has taught their interest to rustle,

    And trained dim eyes to see.

In a quiet way he has joined his will

    With the doctors' when trails were rough,

He's helped them smooth out many a hill,

    This chap they call McNuff.

In a stellar role on the stage of man

    He plays as his heart dictates,

Portraying scenes that shall e'er demand

    A place in the Hall of Fate.

On duty a charge attendant,

    But with actions that good deeds bring,

With each good deed a pennant,

    As a sad heart learns to sing.

So here's to a booster of lives so drear,

THAT CHAP THEY CALL MCNUFF

And a friend when things are tough,

Drink deep to those who our pleading hear,

Like this chap they call McNuff.

GEBERTIG–A BROTHER TO MEN

In a mansion where tired, shaky mortals

    Are gathered, and treated, and trained,

In the realm of Reception's wide portals,

    Where psychiatrists study the brain,

There is one, though the others are royal,

    Who so feels for those in his ken,

That I call him because of his toils,

    Gebertig-a brother to men.

Men who are wavering and mumbling,

    They who have met with defeat,

Humans whose life Fate is jumbling,

    Who long for health's golden treat.

The tottering, senile old fellow

    He comforts and bids rest awhile.

The G. P. with eyes glaring, yellow

    He meets with a soft knowing smile.

The wildest of thoughts cease their storming,

    And the fire dies out, as he sends

His words like a rainbow of morning,

    Gebertig-a brother to men.

When the Master in that great Reception

    Up where old St. Peter stands

Checks in his book of election,

    As he studies the records at hand,

I know when he reads of some toilers,

    Whose energies ever unbend,

To undo the work of the spoilers,

    Like Gebertig-this brother to men.

He'll smile and the smile half in sadness

    Shall beam for a life-time well-spent.

Will shine with a broad flash of gladness

    As he murmurs; "O be thou content."

They are his comrades and brothers,

    Drifters of uncertain trend;

For them is a fight 'bove the others,

    Gebertig – a brother to men.

"Come to thy rest: Thou shalt listen

    To songs that my chosen will sing.

And the eyes of thy patients shall glisten

73

As the breezes our carols shall bring."

"Come! Oh thou worker now wearied.

Rest in my gay, pearly glens,

Thou hast well earned the right to be cheery

Oh Gebertig, thou brother to men."

Author's Note:

As I have now passed from Doctor Gebertig's direct supervision, I take it for granted that this will not be taken as flattery or a bid for prestige. Dedicated to Doctor Gebertig with the sincere respect of R. D. C.

IN THE HOUSE OF
KADJI SMOO

The bittern boomed it's goodnight call,

    The heron sought its nest,

An eagle flopped off to the cliff,

    The sun sank in the west.

Great ships in dock with anchors down,

    All good folks went to bed,

At the twilight bell the gates of hell

    Were opened in Port Said.

Saturday night on the water-front,

    And pay-day at the docks,

Bright the lights in the gay saloons,

    Frenzied the half-mad flocks.

Brutes who tore· at their money bags,

    And freely the gold poured thru'

And the lid was off at the honkey-tonk,

In the house of Kadji Smoo.

I entered the joint and took a chair,

    At a table, my back to the wall,

And high-balled the dago waiter chap

    To bring me a slug of gall.

When I lifted my head and saw a girl

    Held fast in a drunk Finn's arms

About her lingered a modest air,

    Tho 'twas a deuce of a place for charm.

A wilful wisp of dark-brown hair,

    Was waving at her brow,

Musing, I figured she didn't belong

    To that red-dressed crew somehow.

Her eyes looked tired, her face was drawn,

    And her smile was a mirthless one,

As she danced to the whim of the maudlin Finn

    And was paid when the dance was done.

Something held my watchful eye,

    As she danced thru the smoky haze,

There was something wrong with the picture,

    What it was I couldn't say.

Her depthless eyes oft sought the clock,

    And at last when it pealed out one,

IN THE HOUSE OF KADJI SMOO

She grabbed a ragged scarf from the bar,

    And out of the door she ran.

I made up my mind to follow her,

    For I scented a poem for my pen,

So I sauntered out of the whiskey reek,

    Of the haunt of wandering men.

The girl had entered a little shack,

    In a side-street of the town,

She turned a key in the rusty lock

    And pulled the shades all down.

I wanted to see how the poem would end,

    So I crawled lo the rear of the house,

And peeped thru a crack in the kitchen wall,

    I crouched as still as a mouse,

For into the arms of the tired-eyed girl,

    There crept from a rough-board crib,

The tousled heads and sleepy eyes

    Of a couple of laughing kids,

I sneaked away from the kitchen wall,

    And slow walked thru' the night,

Ashamed of my career was I

    As I. thought of a widow's fight.

And now when trouble rends me wild,

And I can't see the heaven blue,

I think of the girl who bared her soul

In the House of Kadji Smoo.

A THOROBRED

When you're tired and dull and dizzy

    And feeling mighty blue,

When the big world is too busy

    Tuh nod or speak tuh you,

Don't it make you feel some better

    When the clouds are low and black

Tuh have a chap break lonesome fetters

    With a slap upon your back?

When a feller starts tuh grinnin',

    Doesn't see your mournful stare,

But starts right in tuh spinnin'

    A joke tuh raise your hair,

He's a friend, pard, don't fergit it

    He's a pal tuh start the pace,

Stick to him, you'll not regret it.

    He's a thorobred in life's race.

GUARDIAN OF THE NIGHT

Softly gliding down the hallway

    Comes that little nurse,

Bringing peace to tossing ill ones,

    Wealth from mercy's purse.

Flitting noiseless as a shadow

    Such a little form,

Gentle, low-voiced, yet such wonders

    By her aid are born.

"Dark-haired, deep-eyed little guardian,

    Can I have just one more drink?

Something hurts me, burns and tears me,

    Can you help me, do you think?"

Such the pleadings she must answer,

    Glad she gives her very best,

And ere long the restless sufferer,

    Peaceful sinks to healthful rest.

GUARDIAN OF THE NIGHT

I have watched her, 'mongst the shadows,

    Flitting here and there,

Duty always time demanding,

    Sick ones need her care.

Hurrying, trotting, uncomplaining,

    Helping Jims or Johns,

Never has she grudged her efforts,

    To the lives in pawn.

Carry on, oh, little guardian,

    May your gentle smile,

Cheer on others as it's boosted

    Us on through dark stiles.

Carry on, your spirit urges

    All of us to win

Through dark, gloomy nights of sickness,

    When all hope is dim.

May you breast all lifetime's sorrows,

    With that spirit glad in store,

May you reap the golden harvest,

    Sown in Reception's Number Four.

Author's Note:

Composed for and about 'Miss Doris Hodge, Night Supervisor in the Reception Building.
Inspired by the way in which she did her best to aid the patients in her care.

VALLEY OF PASSING MEN

There's a dim, arrow valley of sadness,

    Where pain watches over the ward,

Where there's never a whisper of gladness,

    And Death stands with ready sword,

Where dreary the intervaled stillness.

    And mournful grief ever attend

To the wrecks in the last grip of illness,

    In this Valley of Passing Men.

Somehow there's a sigh in one's breathing,

    It seems you can see despair

Like a boiling pot vapor seething,

    And you feel like mumbling a prayer.

It chills your bones to the marrow.

    When a life nears its earthly end,

Sometimes it darts like an arrow,

    In this Valley of Passing Men.

VALLEY OF PASSING MEN

Sadness floats over the being,

    Who enters that surly Ward Ten,

The spirits of tired humans fleeing

    From troubles that seem without end.

I watched one mortal going

    Out on his last great ride,

Watched as with life-blood flowing.

    He floated on ebbing tide.

With the nurse there close beside him,

    As God swung the gates again,

He passed with naught to deride him,

    From the Valley of Passing Men.

So they pass from our sight and their sorrows

    To the land of the pearly moors,

Thru the morgue when they'd hoped tomorrow

    To transfer to out-going Ward Four.

Life is a gamble: two aces

    Are naught if you hold three tens,

So laugh, tho there's death in your faces,

    In the Valley of Passing Men.

THE WHIM OF A
DANCING GIRL

'Twas down at the Sign of the One-Eyed Snake,

    A joint that was never closed.

How many souls had said good-bye

    'Neath its ceiling no one knows.

A ten-foot bar and a couple of bums

    Who tickled the ivory keys

Of a music box that had twanged its notes

    Over the seven seas.

With the freighters loading at busy docks,

    With money and dope and gin,

At the sign of the roiling One-Eyed Snake

    Out there at the topic's brim.

Into the bar with a sailor's weave

    Swung Hans with the jolly eye,

And ordered a round of drinks for the house,

And the slant-eyed waiters fly.

A dancing girl with an eye for art.

    And a love for the things that gleam,

Crept to the side of a sailor Hans

    And offered a toast to the beams.

Drank a toast to a sailor lad,

    A sailor who liked his fun,

But it seemed a dare was in her eyes,

    A dare to an unseen one.

The blue-eyed son of the Holland dikes

    With his rumpled, flaxen hair,

Smiled back deep, and the smile was seen

    By Desperate Turk Bellaire.

Back in the corner with cap pulled low,

    Half covering his green pig eyes,

The killer crouched like a waiting beast,

    And snarled at the dancer's prize.

A jealous gleam like a tiger's glare

    Flashed out 'neath his bushy brows,

A gripping chill crept everywhere.

    As he leered at the motley crowd.

But Hans the brawny knew not of

    The Desperate Turk Bellaire,

Nor that the trifling dancing girl

    Had set the staging there.

So he danced with the faithless gray-eyed dame,

    And drank to the music's time,

Till the midnight hour crept along

    And twelve from the town clock chimed.

The girl and Hans stood at the bar

    Drinking wine of antique brand,

When the girl was swung like a human top

    Clutched in a hairy hand.

Over her towered a brute gone mad,

    A beast by a trifler teased.

The brute was ready to tear, to kill,

    As he threw the girl to her knees.

Then he drew his knife, Hans dropped his glass,

    And as lightning darts thro' the air,

Hans the sailor launched his form

    At the Desperate Turk Bellaire.

The blue steel blade flashed once, and lo!

    The Dutch lad sprawled out still,

Died like a hero, and breathed his last

    Obeying a woman's will.

The dancing dame looked down at Hans

THE WHIM OF A DANCING GIRL

With indifferent calloused stare,

Then crept with a smile to the ape-like arms

Of Desperate Turk Bellaire.

We men are wise, as fools are wise,

And our chances to learn are slim,

For we watch them cry, and hear them sigh,

But we just can't figure their whims.

OVER THE HILL TO NUNN'S

Over a hill thru a forest,

    And over a gurgling brook.

I was nervous and worried and shaky

    When first that journey I took.

With a group of close-watched patients

    I trudged and my life seemed done.

With hopeless heart and mind inflamed

    I went over the hill to Nunn's.

So oft since then I've trod that trail

    To that friendly little store

Where we purchase smokes and candy

    And forget our iron-barred door.

While strolling thru the forest,

    We rollicked in jokes and fun,

As we hiked o'er trail of sunshine

    On over the hill to Nunn's.

The mumbling pals who made that trip

Have all come safely thru.

Strong and well they're home once more

Excepting one or two.

Poor Bill has died as the drunkard dies,

And I on North-Two-One

Am the only one of that R.B. crew

Who travels the hill to Nunn's.

And sometime now in the twilight

When evening so peaceful, still,

Settles about with purple cloak,

I can see just topping the hill.

A silent crew of stumbling men

At the bridge where the brooklet runs

Ghosts that rest in the hazel shade,

On the trail that leads to Nunn's.

And now that I am well again,

I love to pause 'neath the trees

At the little bridge where I used to rest

With my pals from the great R. B.

With a grateful heart and a steady step

I stride with new life begun

Along the path where friends have trod

Over the hill to Nunn's.

Requiescat In Pace

Oh foolish being, who dreads the peaceful grave,

    Who fears to die, let your wild heart be brave,

'Tis but a single moment's time and you are borne

    To happiness. where joy is ne'er enslaved.

Fie! Fie! believe you not the Good Book's written word?

    Can you not revel in what you have heard

Of that great Master who has promised to be there

    To welcome every mortal, flower and bird?

When in the peaceful quiet of midnight hour,

    Close wearied eyes and enter sacred bower

Of loving heart's communion with Him there,

    There'll rush to your weak soul His thrilling power.

Ah, I have been so wicked, what sins I've done!

    In shame I bow my head. Can I be one

Who cleansed by Him, dwell in His love forgiven?

    Ah yes, I see His promise in the sun.

REQUIESCAT IN PACE

So oft I've sinned against his pure grace,

    That mayhap down in hell should be my place.

But now in true repentance loud I cry,

    And He forgives me as I leave the sinner's race.

Alone, with night's majestic gown,

    I lift my heart to sing with silent rounds

His praises, and what can Death mean to me?

    One step toward Him that grassy church-yard mound.

So rest ye well, oh heart that's filled with fear

    To bear you on, His angels linger near.

One sigh, soft farewells and you float away

    With just a memory lying on the bier.

THE DREAMER

Three buds together sprang from out the ground,

    Within a church-yard 'mongst the sacred mounds.

Two of the buds burst out in blossoms sweet and fair,

    The third turned out a thistle bold and brown.

Three brothers grew up in a cultured home;

    One of them was fain the world to roam,

The second grew a home-town business man,

    The third, ah, he was but a dreaming drone.

The wanderer laughed in robust muscled health,

    The business man gained lands and glittering wealth.

The dreamer smiled and sang of beauteous dreams,

    And time crept on with never ceasing stealth.

The wanderer mated with an Indian's life,

    The business man brought home a comely wife.

The dreamer said "Ah, mating's not for me,

    I would not drag a maiden thru blind strife."

THE DREAMER

"Fool! Fool!" his friends and parents grieving cried,

"That you alone should face life's lonely tide."

The dreamer asked "Shall I before my God make vows

That I may break because of wilful bride?"

"Shall I help bring a child into the world

Then see it by court to orphan's refuge hurled,

Because my wife and I found we were wrong?"

In dying could I face those gates of pearl

"That I would sometime enter when God calls,

And I leave this weak, ashy body fall

Back to the earth from whence it came to me?

Ah no I want no bitter cup of gall".

And bidding love begone be wrote his own bright dreams

In rhymes and sent them out in gladdening beams.

To cheer the saddened souls out in a sorrowed world,

Still smiling, he was sent where madman's wild eyes gleam.

THE COME-BACK

Marcus Curry—does that name bring a vision to your mind?

A countless group of human forms, of lines and lines and lines

Of sorrowed folk who bowed in grief their wearied, worried heads,

And learned to live with hope renewed as health to them was sped.

A doctor,—ah, how much of good do those six letters spell,

Peace and health and mercy where life had been a hell,

Of fear and gloom and sullenness and grief and aching pains,

The demons that destroy a mind and hector staggering brains.

Could I drift back across the smoky hills of life, I'd be

A doctor to the myriad ills of frail humanity,

Just as this Doctor Curry takes his fearless, sincere stand

Against the joy-destroying scourge of our own stricken land

And as I pass his office in the Center's cavelike yawn,

I bow my head; a sincere soul's salute for him is drawn.

From my tired heart a grateful throb booms out in silent peals,

My homage to a chieftain great who others' sorrow feels.

THE COME-BACK

I'm just a drunk, a has-been, but once I'd set a pace,

Once I had led in famed career, but ere the gloried race

Was more than half way run, I failed and faltered, lower fell,

Then shamed, I sought to drown out woe 'neath liquor's numbing spell.

On down and down till with the mind and health destroying flow

I floated through life's gutters, a clown in lifetime's show,

A clown with bearded, scarred-up face and battered, homely mein,

Who clutched a scimitar and crescent and buried honored name,

The only clean thought in my mind, "The compass and the square,"

The noble good they stood for and the four gates opened there.

But for the rest my mind was blank or torn or burned and shaken,

For I wasn't even sure of how many years were taken

From out the pages of my life. I only sought to pump

The barrel of fiery poison dry, then creep out to life's dump

To die, alone, unchided by a slow death at my throat,

A nameless rambler with a pin of honor on his coat.

A symbol earned by being raised at that great eastern gate,

How bright it gleams, tho' it was worn by weakened pawn of fate.

And now that I have viewed so oft the restless world in play

At work and study, know it's night and understand it's day.

I've wandered to this refuge-God's haven for the ill.

Where Marcus Curry strives to heal on Greystone's peaceful hill.

I faced the earnest, quizzing eyes of the psychiatric staff.

No one scorned my faltering speech nor at my history laughed.

So strange it seemed that I should find a loyal brotherhood,

Who knew I meant the world no ill, who really understood.

They sent me to a parlor ward where the battle was begun,

As I gathered up the pieces 'twixt the walls of North Three-One.

They treated me and cleansed me of the whiskey and the gin,

Then, wonder of all wonders, they cleansed the heart within.

They scrubbed and scoured and straightened the tangles of my mind,

They made of me an editor and let me fashion rhymes.

They've built me up and bucked me up, till now the dawning morn

In crowning beauty lingers like the sound of golden horns.

There's hope within my bosom and I want to fight again

Thru' the charging tide of conquest in the outer world of men.

I feel a steely calmness where I once in frenzy shook,

And I long to test the temper in a being long forsook.

I want to swing a saddle to a mustang once again,

And I want to trail a panther thru' uncharted mountain glens.

I want to face real danger with a ten-foot iron-spiked pole,

And ride the king-log thru' a jam and thru' the rapids' roll.

I want to toss my blanket on some copra-smelling ship,

And fight a storm-torn canvas on a South Sea Island trip,

I want to sniff salt zephyrs in a nipa-covered shack;

I wonder if Alethra will be there when I get back,—

THE COME-BACK

To cook my rice and spear the fish und place within my reach

A gourd full of fermenti, as I doze there on the beach.

I want to tramp Brazilian jungles, and brave the fever's curse,

Where it's manhood that must conquer and the weakest drop the first.

I want to sample danger, and at terror once more laugh

I was granted something I had lost; by Doctor Curry's staff.

I want to toss some silver to a beggar in Port Said,

And trek across Sahara with a sand dune for a bed.

I thought that I was almost done with traveling trails of strife,

But a year at good old Greystone has granted newer life.

I want to pit my puny strength 'gainst any odds and, see

Just what those mental doctors have gone and done for me.

I'm going to help my fellowmen in every way I can,

I owe it to the living world, so strong I take my stand.

And at the sunset when God calls for me to go beyond,

A prayer shall filter thru' the dusk, of passing vagabond.

If you see a comet shooting thru' the firmament of blue,

You can say it's the reflection as R. D. C. went thru'.

ODE TO ONE OF OUR LITTLE ONES

"Nameless, fatherless," who dares these words exclaim,

Of this wee babe so free of sin and blame?

Who dares to judge how legal be his birth,

Who dares begrudge him life of joy and mirth?

A name, what means a name down here below,

When on God's record book the writing shows

That this dear babe was lent to us a while

To grant the aged, sorrowed ones a smile?

Shame, 'tis you, ah! world, who should be shamed,

Who scorns a small new player in life's game.

Unfold the blanket, faded, patched and torn,

And let this precious mortal greet the morn.

Oh! world, turn not thy glance of Puritanic scorn

On this bright gem of life's dew-glistening morn.

To him and his bright mother offer friendly hand,

ODE TO ONE OF OUR LITTLE ONES

They have so few friends in this pretentious land.

What matter if the mother sinned? Art thou a god?

Do ye know well the path thy son has trod?

Judge not, lest some day judgment come to you;

In bitter tears your sentence you may rue.

Fatherless, and shall the fact bring harm

To this wee babe whom God would take in arms

And fondle, oh! so much more tenderly

Than He would ever do for you or me?

Bear him a merry smile, as wondering there he lies,

He who's destined to hear so little praise;

Bid him be happy and let on the message go

That he is here, and God would have it so.

ADOLPH THE BARBER

Line up, lads; this is barbering day,

Leave your books and your work and play,

Climb into the chair, let your cares drift away;

For Adolph the barber is shaving to-day.

Come on, all you patients, bid farewell to fun,

The first to be lathered the first to be done.

Your whiskers must go that neatness shall stay,

For Adolph the· master is shaving to-day.

Recline in the chair, your head on the rest,

Peaceful the heart that beats in your breast,

Making you cleaner to win in life's fray,

Adolph the barber is shaving to-day.

For years he has offered his heart's very best

That helpless ones may be by cleanliness blest,

Shaving and snipping the hours away,

Adolph the barber is shaving to-day.

ADOLPH THE BARBER

Some day when the Master who watches up there

Looks down on our haven, he'll smjle thru' his cares,

And whisper so gently, "Come, Adolph, and play,

You've done well my will; no more shaving to-day."

And there's many of us who must dwell 'twixt these walls

Will pause and reflect and a teal drop will fall.

"He gave us much comfort," each patient will say,

But Adolph the barber's not shaving to-day.

MEMORIES

Back o'er the dimming trails of yesteryears,

    Where visions blend with visions of the past,

Some bright with songs and laughter, some with tears

    Are filled, and yet their grief but moments lasts.

That old farmhouse beside the thorny hedge,

    The lower pasture where you roamed a boy,

The orchard and the great barn where was wedged

    The swings, the ladders, everything that brought you joy.

A mother's patient, smiling, roseate face,

    And sisters three God, can it be they're old?

All married, gone from that snug, cozy place

    Where your first ghost and fairy tales were told.

Your father, just a little old and grey,

    Whose jokes and puns at parties famed him far,

Your brother, now he's wandered far away,

    Reflective, you turn back o'er memory's bar.

MEMORIES

Those wondrous days were only incidental then,

But now how sweet and grand 'twould be

Could you but wander thru' them once again

And be a little child at mother's knee.

SONG OF A DIZZY ONE

This is the song of a dizzy one,

    A lad of erratic ken,

Who got mixed up in the scheme of things,

    Out in the world of men.

Who wanted to die, who longed to die,

    But God wouldn't tell him when.

Up there on North Three-One he sang,

    Pressed close to the chilly bars,

How those echoes sobbed and rang,

    As he mourned to the night and the stars,

Mourned for ghosts of the loving ones,

    Who'd passed by the beacon Mars.

A song off key and somewhat strained,

    'Twas pretty well out of tune,

And he shook as he warbled that queer refrain,

    Of the girl who loved a loon,

And his pale eyes flashed and seemed to crash,

 As he raved of a honeymoon.

With a leg gone lame, and a half cocked eye,

 And arms like a windmill's fan,

With a homely phiz, he would send his cry

 Down to the road of man.

His dull eyes gleamed, like a witch's sheen,

 But the world couldn't understand.

Sang calling a woman, to leave the night,

 And glide to his lone arms' fold,

God! but his face was a fearful sight,

 'Twould make your blood run cold,

As the madman saw that his hopes were slight,

 And his face was yellow and old.

Now he softly whispered the name "Elaine",

 He wheezed as he gasped the word,

Like the dying plea of a soul in pain,

 And surely his God had heard,

For he staggered back from the window pane,

 Dropped dead, and his wild eyes blurred.

Yes this is a song of a dizzy one,

 A soul with erratic ken,

One of the guys that lost his love,

Out in the world of men,

And ·had his account marked "Paid in full"

By the stroke of immortal pen.

LET THIS BE NAMELESS

I scribbled a crude-rhyming verse

    Of a man who had proved my friend;

Gave from a word-poor purse,

    But 'twas sincere, beginning to end.

'Twas a poem of a medical man,

    Who granted me liberty's goal,

Who had taught me to say "I can"

    With the faltering voice of my soul.

And the portrait I painted was sent

    To the wife of the merciful man.

It brought her a smile of content,

    Caused her heart with joy to expand.

And tho' I must languish and pine

    In the gloom of an outcast's cell.

The thought of that smile divine

    Shall ring like a tocsin bell.

For tho' I am heavy with sin,

    God knows in His heart all the while

That I wrote with a gift from Him,

    And brought a good woman a smile.

The Guarded Ones

A shuffling, scraping, stumbling line

    Is pushing down the hall

Unkempt and snarling, fierce, they grin

    Between the greystone walls.

What is that aimless, tramping horde

    With the white coats at their heels?

It's the guarded ones from the section wards

    On their way to the evening meal.

Limping, swaying, pushing on,

    Eyes cast to the floor,

The violent patients mushing on,

    And staggering thru' the doors.

With hopeless gaze and deadened hearts

    They surge and dart and reel,

Tho' illness bade their minds depart,

    Their bodies call for meals.

Here's a lad of tender age

    With head hung on his chest,

Not long ago, on' young life's page

    He slept on his mother's breast

Now with hope and joy far gone,

    He sorrow nor pleasure feels,

He treads in the rank of the wards beyond,

    On his way to the evening meal.

There labors a grey-haired, aged one,

    With an attendant at either side.

Soon his last long march is done,

    And he goes on that last still ride.

Even now the white coats bear his weight

    As his brain in madness reels,

The attendants know that soon wierd Fate

    Will bear him from his meals.

There they go through the shadows,

    Like ghosts thru' a forest of pines,

And all in the spirit of pathos,

    Vanish the straggling lines.

Only echoes resounding

    'Twixt the yellowed, yawning walls,

Only memories dwell around

THE GUARDED ONES

The stretching shiny halls.

Gone the hopeless patients now

With their guardians at their heels.

God have mercy on their brows,

Bring peace to minds that reel.

ALWAYS LIKE THIS

I want to get well, but I can't, it seems,

And I'm still disturbed in· my restless

        dreams,

And I just can't catch the sunlight's beams.

    Will it always be like this?

There's something ·bothers me all night

It hectors, taunts till the morning's light,

And the mirror shows me a sorry sight.

    Will I always look like this?

I try to do just as the doctors say

And do it all in the proper way,

But still I drag on thru' listless days.

    Will all days be like this?

But one thing sure, there's room for a grave

On the old home ranch where the free

        winds rave,

And its one long rest, with sorrow saved,

    Then it will not be like this.

I'm sick of the hustling to and fro,

And I want to go where there is no woe,

But I don't dare tell the doctor so,

    That things are so amiss,

For he'd give me a funny look,

And write me up in a black-bound book

Where the suicidal notes are took,

    I'd be much worse off than this.

OMNIPOTENCE DIVINE

Tonight a superb inspiration flows

   To my poor pen which carves of torture's throes,

But words are weak. I grope in lingua's haze

   To find the crayons that can wondrous thoughts

      disclose.

In this brief maelstrom of existence we call life.

   Of great careers that have borne on thru' strife,

Of warriors, statesmen, martyrs; not one's brought the good

   To humans as has nurse of mercy rife.

To ease the suffering ones, to banish racking pains,

   To grant sweet rest to quiet blazing brains,

What could be grander; nobler, more sublime,

   Than to live life that bids, "Go forth in joy

      again?"

And as memory floats before my mental eye,

   I probe and search for words that can imply

A salutation to a leader of the clan,

 Who serve in sickened hours-nor let their

  service die.

Upon a throne where Greystone's velvet lawns

 Are spread for wearied, wandering feet to tread,

The great inspirant of this humble work

 Rules in career that Jesus smiles upon.

With crown of silvery hair by honor's touch,

 A placid face serene that murmur much

Of pence and health to countless suffering ones,

 Tho they be ill of mind or grasping padded

  crutch,

A life of fulsome years yet speaking not of age,

 A priceless book and on each day's recorded page

A deed of mercy, a life or mayhap ten

 Was granted rest and peace its worth ungauged.

How you must rest at set of evening sun,

 How sweet your thoughts, counting one by one

The sickened souls you've helped that day to ease,

 They form a rosary, these things that you have

  done.

Of you and your famed clan, this pen of mine

 Is helpless to so glorify its scrawling lines

As I should wish. So of you to the world I'll send,

With truth 'tis said Omnipotence Divine.

Author's Note:

Just another of my mind pictures woven about Mrs. Anne. How, our Superintendent of Nurses.

To All those who aid and comfort the helpless sick I render sincere homage. To continue it is the greatest career that I know of.

Through The Shadows

A creaking door and a soft-turned key

    A starchy rustles comes to me,

A quiet pit-pat bring to my ear

    The fact that the night nurse hovers near.

Midnight chimes from the faithful clock;

    It cheers with its steady low tick-tock

And a smile seems sent from its face profound

    As the loyal nurse starts on her rounds.

Each night she comes thru' the sleeping wards

    Her footsteps beating the same soft chord.

With a cheery word and a friendly smile

    She drives away the day's drear trials.

And as I sit on North-Two-One,

    Scribbling rhymes for the months to come,

Her passing seems to me a sign

    That greater worth shall bless my lines.

For tho' my text in rhyme be blurred,

    Its real intent is Just like hers

She toils to watch o'er sickened throngs.

    While I would fashion for them songs.

To brighten up their somber plight,

    Alas! all I can do is write,

While she can drive away their pain,

    Her labors never are in vain.

Now she passes from my ken

    And I take up inspired pen.

To carve out one more rambling rhyme,

    Of her, as she swings down the line.

Lead on, Oh Pal of wearied crew,

    There's many wish the best for you.

And may your daughter understand

    Her mother gives her spirit's brand.

Unto the wondering, helpless ones,

    Who, suffering, still smile when she comes

And I know of no honor grand,

    That can compare to "friend to man."

There's something noble in her face

    As she walks on in patient grace.

Through stretching halls, till burst of dawn

On she travels, on, and on.

Author's Note:

The above is inspired by the untiring efforts with which the Night Superintendent Mrs. Patricia Bradshaw, watches over the patients under her care.

THE WORLD SHALL KNOW

Where peaceful, thriving Morristown extends dominions wide,

Its lordly roads and avenues of shady, tree-blessed pride,

Where vari-colored gardens bloom in radiance arrayed

To give the night aroma and to cheer the drab, dull day,

There dwells a worthy leader, one who guides his clan

And swings the probing, watchful minds of sincere thinking spans,

Who from his heart's core offers up straightforward, clean-purged

thought,

That for the dwellers of the land a world of good has wrought.

A man of men, a justful man, with no pretentious airs,

Whose deeds are as he meets your gaze, calm, level, on the square.

He has no taunting mud to throw, no Judas axe to grind,

Be you a prince or beggar, unprejudiced his mind.

And because he faces shell and gas and sabre's slashing thrust

For others who have placed in him their hallowed faith and trust,

I creep close to the moonlight's beam that smiles thru' rusty bars

THE WORLD SHALL KNOW

And carve this inspiration; and the wise old friendly stars

Seem to twinkle deeper wisdom then, as tho' they understood

That mortals felt the thoughts I penned, that Coggeshall was good,

Was true and sincere to his clan who placed him on the throne

To guard their interests in the mart, protect the people's own.

A radiant, joy-gyrating thought flowed thru' my leaky pen

Of things he'd done and caused to be while serving fellowmen,

By casting grafting parasites from public office hold

And proving to his subjects that safe he'd kept their gold.

Not filthy, yellow muck alone, but greater worth in fold,

Of decent schools, of cleaner shows, that finer tales be told.

I hear that he is friend to weak and sick who throng life's lanes,

I hear that he is eager to banish groans and pains.

They say that tho' he likes to hear the opera's cultured voice,

To hear a song from orphan's home for him is better choice.

A subtle God-sent vision unfolds before my mind,

That Murray Coggeshall shall yet rule those of greater line.

That he is destined to guide our steps from chieftain's chair.

Where Justice guards the portals and Mercy guards the stairs.

Could this demented rhymer cast one last vote for his land,

'Twould be for Murray Coggeshall, for one who's proved A MAN.

But hark, the night attendant nears, I must steal back to bed,

My message is by far too crude, perhaps the stars instead

Of me will let the people know, of faithful brotherhood

That wisely have they chosen, for Coggeshall is good.

And as I march down yawning halls, entrained with mumbling men,

A safe, secure feeling that protected is our trend

Comes to my helpless longing heart. The way don't seem so dark

To know that folks like Coggeshall are friends of Greystone Park.

Author's Note:

Just a rhyme that was so clearly and forcibly inspired by what I had read and heard of Mr. Coggeshall that I could not sleep until it was written out.

LAIRD OF THE LANCE

There's a snowy white room in the Clinic

    Where silence supreme rules the air.

Measured each action and movement,

    There's the tension of hope and despair.

As a surgeon leans over a patient

    Clasping a thin, shiny knife,

Doctor Collins reporting for duty,

    To carve for the sake of a life.

Loudly the clock screams its seconds,

    Tense, steady nurses who wait

The nod or the beck of the surgeon

    As be pits his best knowledge 'gainst Fate.

Lips in a straight line of grimness,

    His heart like a drum to a fife,

Fingers like wands of tried magic,

    Collins with merciful knife.

A moan trembles pitiful, sobbing,

    A sound half a sigh, half a prayer,

Then silence-ah! now he is pausing

    With scalpel extended in air.

He looks on his work. Satisfaction

    Is plain on his unworried face.

Successful the dread operation,

    A life again swings in the race.

Decisive and quiet his manner.

    He has won with skill against chance.

Magic he's worked with a scalpel,

    This miracle man of the lance.

THE LOW-BROW

She's not the slightest bit pretty,

    Her carriage is straight as a post,

She's not even brilliant nor witty:

    Plain, you would call her at most.

She's not even blessed with complexion,

    She doesn't use make-up you see,

Her smile is of quiet subjection,

    But someway it glorifies me.

Her slippers have never seen Paris,

    Her stockings may have several runs,

Her hair-may Dame Fashion spare us—

    In a great Grecian bundle is done.

Not costly her garments but somehow

    They speak of a clean heart within,

And tho she be rated a low-brow,

    I'll bet she knows little of sin.

A dead one most flappers would call her

  A flat tire, well yes, perhaps,

But men meeting her, walk the straighter

  And their hands go right to their caps.

Carry on, little low-brow, I greet you,

  With a world trotting skeptic's salute.

No sorrow can ever defeat you,

  Tho your lips of bright sayings be mute.

Bear on thru age frolic-covered.

  Your spirit its message will send

To the heart of some staunch, noble lover

  Who roams in the meadows of men.

LA LONGUE TRAVERSE

Oh Nursie, tell me Nursie

    What is that ceaseless beat.

Like the hollow tramping, tramping

    Of a hundred million feet?

It seems it's all about me,

    It racks my aching head;

Do you think it is my buddies

    In the land of soldier dead?

Oh it's boom, boom, boom!

    Like tocsin peals of doom,

A host of silent spirits

    Trudging onward thru the gloom.

I'm colder, Nurse, I'm colder,

    Won't you please take hold my hand

When I float out in the darkness

    Of that unknown other land?

127

There are voices coming nearer,

    And it seems to me they say,

"We are coming, coming, coming,

    To bear you on your way,"

And that boom, boom, boom!

    To the sick man in the room,

Was the tread of trudging spirits,

    Sent to bear him thru' the gloom.

THE CRYSTAL IN THE BLAZE.

I've been watching, little comrade,

    As you sat a-dreaming there,

I have seen the rays of sunset

    Spread their radiance o'er your hair.

I have paused and drifted backward,

    As I leaned o'er iron gate,

Drifted backward to the prairies,

    Where I first linked arms with Fate.

There at night upon some hillock

    I would build my signal fire,

While the coyotes serenaded

    Sobbing souls in furs attired.

And as I unrolled my blankets

    With my bronch turned out to graze,

I would build my future castles

    In the crystals of the blaze.

129

In those leaping flames I conquered

    Every barrier to fame,

Mastered every art and science,

    Tho' I couldn't write my name.

There I built a pearly mansion

    And a flower garden laid.

Then I peered hard at the fire

    For the face of one true maid.

Sometimes I could glimpse her countenance

    In the twisting, leaping glare,

Faintly smiling she seemed waiting

    For my coming to her there.

But when dawn like rainbowed cyclone

    Burst, I sat in lilac haze,

Just a lonely hoping cowboy,

    Staring wondering at the blaze.

How I loved those nights of watching

    As I sang to resting herds,

Thinking, planning for the future,

    And a fond heart's whispered word.

Knowing not I'd be an outcast

    Ere I'd aged to thirty-five,

That I'd stare from close-barred windows

THE CRYSTAL IN THE BLAZE.

God! what Fate can do with lives.

And one morning as I passed you

    As you worked inside the gate,

It seemed you were staring, gazing

    Through life's windows probing fate.

Something in your manner gripped me

    As you sat in pondering haze,

Just as I had done you wondered

    And sought truth in crystal blaze.

Like you, I was one time hoping

    For the joys that life holds dear,

But now I'm downward sloping

    And the crystal's not so clear.

For you I wish, oh soft-eyed comrade,

    That Fate will ever light the ways,

May you see, and find much glory

    In the crystal of the blaze.

LAUGH WITH JOY AWHILE

Quiet! restless, wakeful, troubled soul,

    What reason do you fret? What terrored goal

Art thou in fear of? Surely 'tis not death.

    For death is but a sleep, a priceless dole.

Pine not, oh heart, but rather sing and smile,

    Cast off thy grief and laugh with joy awhile,

Forget thy baseless fears, while life is here,

    And dance in wild abandon o'er the last few miles.

God does not bid thee wear that melancholy face,

    He sees no pleasure in a sorrow seeking place.

A smile is His endowment, a song His pearl,

    So put aside thy cares, and dance in joyous grace.

Should you fall ill what matter shall it be?

    'Twill make you appreciate good health, its blessing see,

For sorrow is a temperer, that gives a better taste

    To happiness when once again you're strong and free.

THE MOTH AND I

I have hit the trails and caught life's flails,

    I have battled the ocean's brine,

I have played the game of the moth and

        flame,

    And laughed in the face of time.

I have lived on fish on· a chink mud scow,

    Trapped snakes with a South Sea belle.

I've eaten roast dogs with the Tatalogs

    Out beyond the equator's hell.

I've watched a eunuch swing the lash

    On one of the harem queens.

I've seen the human sacrifice

    As a crazed cult's fire gleamed

I have slopped in drink where the Malays

        slink

    Round a nipa shelter's reek,

Rolled in dead drunk with a Sanskrit

    phrase

      Got up with a verse of Greek.

On the beach "Disgrace" with a hairy

    face,

      Tho' with strength like a pampas bull.

I've cursed the world, my mind awhirl

      And my heart with sorrows full.

I've lain on the sands of the darkened

    lands

      Alone, with the sea and sky,

A beach comber bum is the lowest scum,

      And one of the worst was I.

At midnight the will grows weak and still,

      And conscience somehow doesn't sting,

So there I would lie till the first· blush of

    day,

      And of other times I would sing.

And sometimes it seemed like a good

    poet's dream

      As the waves murmured peacefully.

My babies came back from the rough

    mountain shack,

THE MOTH AND I

And they'd tumble and romp over me.

Come to play, 'neath the white moon's

    rays,

    "Merry Winnie" and "Sweet Marie,"

And we'd sing the songs of the days long

    gone,

    And the life that used to be.

They'd nestle there and they had no care,

    Nor quizzed me of what I'd done,

Whether I ranked with the kings of swank,

    Or belonged to the order of bums.

'Neath the great white moon while the life-

    buoy boomed,

    We laughed thru' the past once more.

Two little tikes, so much alike,

    And a wreck on the Fiji shore.

The three of us played in the silvery

    glade,

    And our joy was a sight to see,

It made me forget I was just a wreck,

    In my dreams of the "used-to-be."

Thru' the quiet, starry night till the ·pale,

    streaked light

Of glorious crashing dawn,

My darlings danced till the darkness was

blanched,

Then they whispered goodbye and were

gone.

So I bound up my roll, got a job passing

coal,

Back to the old U. S. A.

There's the spirit of God in that good old

sod,

And you just can't stay away.

The years rolled on and Fortune spawned,

And I drew not a sober breath

Till I sat there stunned oii North Three

One,

All packed for a trip to death,

Yes, I've played the game of the moth

and flame,

We've both got to singe and die,

The moth lies cramped in a coal-oil lamp,

In a hospital morgue lay I.

THE SHIP OF STATE

The loyal ship *New Jersey* sailed thru' ocean gates,

    And lifted great white sails above its mighty bows,

Launched forth with decks and berths of precious freight,

    And for the main she cleared with spray-splashed prow.

Across the world of blue she made her way,

    Straight out across the summer of the world,

And honor's emblem from her masthead played,

    And justice's myriad banners all unfurled.

About the decks of this great, sturdy ship

    Children played and laughed aloud in glee,

Aged humans in full peace, upon the trip

    Felt safe, secure, their hearts and minds at ease.

For though the typhoon's angry, treacherous breath

    Strained at its best, it could not thwart the minds

That steered this ship *New Jersey* clear of death,

    And let it onward rock, the hurricane behind.

Such was the faith of those who made their home

    On ship that well has stood the acid test,

The stately craft that like the restful gloam

    Floats in with peaceful mien, from out the west.

Up in the pilot house with grave, set face

    The Captain stood and peered out o'er the sea,

And close beside him in the navigator's place

    There crouched a man tense with sincerity.

And as a reef is neared, an unseen danger gives retort,

    Shows his chart, the navigator would the captain touch

And quietly speak, "Two points right hard to port."

    And when they'd passed, remark, "This coast abounds in

        such."

The navigator holds in his own hands the fate

    Of those who trust their dear ones to the craft,

His brain dares not grow tired, for should he speak too late,

    Would come the fatal crash, and haunting demons laugh.

So navigator of our royal, sovereign ship,

    We're glad that we chose you to see us through,

And well you've kept your vigil on the trips,

    That we entrust our coin and peace to you.

Forge on, Frank Abel, through the waves of graft,

    And aid our troubled waters, cleanse the people-robbing

dens.

Bring honest chiefs to offices where grafters laugh,

And we will back you with our votes again.

THE HARD RIDING KID OF BAR T.

Sometimes as I sit in my office,

    And the presses are printing my rhymes,

I drift back o'er the years of the locust,

    And live in the great olden times.

I can see the bronchos I've broken

    I can look o'er some battles and smiles,

As the past comes again to my vision,

    And I ramble o'er memory's miles.

And as scenes from the West and the Border

    Unroll, I can see on his knees

A lad whom I brand as a hero,

    The Hard Riding Kid of Bar T.

Just a tramp who'd forsaken the railroad,

    Dirty and lousy and such,

Shifty-eyed; bred in the city,

THE HARD RIDING KID OF BAR T.

He didn't size up very much.

He knocked at the door of the bunkhouse

And asked for some chow and a job.

He blinked as tho' ready to crumble,

And his voice sounded much like a sob.

Dad gave him some grub and he wolfed it,

Gosh! but he put it away,

And I nodded the old man to hire him

To help us stack wintering hay.

The kid caught the nod and he brightened,

And followed me out to the barn

Where we rolled up a smoke and he told me

The blamedest, all-firedest of yarns.

He had broken from his close herding daddy,

And run far away from his home,

Taken up with some bums and then drifted

To the West, where he'd heard rustlers roamed.

Some way there were tears in his story

As he told of the wrongs he had done,

Just a kid, and some old mother's glory,

Who waited for news of her son.

It seemed that the sheriff was looking

For him all over the East.

He didn't dare wander back yonder,

    They'd gather him in at the least.

I looked the kid over right careful,

    And I pitied the poor skinny cuss;

I made up my mind I would back him

    If it ever came up to a muss.

So I rigged him an outfit discarded,

    And roped him a plumb gentle hoss,

And a six gun my buddy had carried

    Before Mexican Pete won the toss.

The youngster climbed into the saddle,

    Then up went his finely shaped head,

"From now on I am being a man, Sir",

    By gosh! that's just what he said.

It sure did tickle me plenty

    To hear him 'low he'd play it fair,

And I felt like I wanted to holler

    That miracles still sometimes flared.

But I gave him a clamp on the shoulder,

    And we rode for the mesa that day,

Sizing the crop for the mowers,

    And keeping an eye out for strays.

I showed the kid all about roping

And how to take care of his hoss,

How to balance himself in the saddle

If a broncho tried pitching a toss.

He had nerve, I could see by his manner,

And pride as his squareness I'd see,

So I dubbed him with monicker glowing

As the Hard Riding Kid of Bar T.

The nickname just tickled him silly,

For a minute then, strange to my ken,

He gulped and cast his eyes downward,

Then strode from the dumfounded men.

But I told all the riders the story,

And a thundering roar split the air,

For the Hard Riding Kid was their pardner,

And they saw that he meant to be fair.

And the kid-man, oh, man how triumphed!

And plumb tickled me blind as a flea,

As I saw what a man he was becoming,

This Hard Riding Kid of Bar T.

That fall we hit out for the mountains

To round up some maverick strays,

The Kid and I rolled up our blankets,

The trip took a couple of days.

143

And we rode where few white men had ridden,

    Where a slip meant a goodnight call,

But oh, it was glorious, peaceful,

    And how I was bound to it all!

The trail led thru' canyon's of cedars,

    And the brow of a cliff thick with pines,

Grass velvet and purply garbing

    The slopes where cattle trails wind.

The peace of the forest about us,

    I reveled in unfettered glee,

On over the Paso Diablo

    With the Hard Riding Kid of Bar T.

We were hugging a cliff of the canyon,

    And the river a half mile straight down

To our sight looked as wide as a ribbon,

    A ribbon of dull, muddy brown.

At the narrowest point of the paso

    My branch shied, a rattler had sprung,

And I sailed thru' the air down the cliffside

    Then I caught on a one word and hung.

There with the rocks far below me,

    And death if that frail root gave way,

Clutching and fearful of breathing,

THE HARD RIDING KID OF BAR T.

I thought 'twas the end of my days.

But the Kid was standing above me

    With a lariat coiled in his hand,

Trying to get my location,

    So I hollered that he'd understand.

He threw down the rope, but the distance

    Was too far, and the mocking of Fate

Seemed to laugh at my torturing, clutching,

    And my teeth were beginning to grate.

The sweetroot that held me was slipping,

    Slowly but surely it gave,

Letting me nearer and nearer

    The crash to the watery grave.

But just when my hope seemed the darkest,

    I saw that blamed Kid coming down,

Hand over hand down the lasso,

    And carefully feeling his ground

Three thousand feet to the bottom,

    And he on a half-inch line,

With something that crept down my cheekbones

    I lauded that buddy of mine.

With the chances of hell all against him,

    And risking his young life for me,

God! what a spirit was in him,

 This Hard Riding Kid of Bar T.

Well, he anchored to rock and then cast me

 Another long rope, and it fell

Straight to my grasp, and I tell you

 I hollered a mighty glad yell.

I climbed up the rope to the cliff-brim

 The Kid still anchoring the line.

Then made fast to a boulder

 And advised the Kid to take his own time.

A groan from the cliffside aroused me

 And I crawled to the brink of the brim,

I chilled as I saw what had happened,

 And sickened, my eyesight grew dim.

For the kid was gasping and dying,

 A rattlesnake grasped in his hand,

But he cried as the venom was killing,

 "Tell mother I died like a man."

In a minute the story was ended,

 He passed and his spirit was freed,

Giving his life for a comrade,

 The Hard Riding Kid of Bar T.

We buried him out on the mesa,

THE HARD RIDING KID OF BAR T.

Where he once loved to bet on the red,

With his spurs and his blankets beside him

And a crude cross of pine at his head.

And of friends that I've made in my travel

Not one's meant as much to me

As the boy who came and the man who died,

That Hard Riding Kid of Bar T.

Have on, O western cyclones,

Blaze out, O lightning's flash;

Bring back to men who've fought you fair

Nor trembled at your crash.

The story of the wandering lad

Who, calm, faced eternity,

And spoke his last of his Mother,

The Hard Riding, Kid of Bar T.

GREYSTONE'S HOLY NIGHT

'Twas in a great hospital

    One gladsome Christmas eve,

We gathered in the ballroom

    Around the sparkling tree.

We saw a gloried pageant,

    Heard carols gaily sang.

How the chorus reverberated

    As we joined the glad refrain.

There was joy on every countenance,

    Every heart was free and light,

Glory, goodwill, peace and laughter

    Reigned at Greystone's Holy Night,

"Why should I call that night holy?"

    If you could have seen the looks

That leaped from happy faces

    As they clutched their carol books,

GREYSTONE'S HOLY NIGHT

You would say, "The spirit of Jesus

    Must be floating everywhere,"

As they sat and eyed those presents,

    In their eyes a thankful prayer.

Some had only come to Greystone,

    Many lingered there for years.

Some would soon be well, and leaving

    Others doomed to dwell in fear.

But to-night they all were happy,

    Not a sign of sorrow's blight;

And they laughed, and talked, and warbled

    There on Greystone's Holy Night.

With the sound of sleigh bells ringing

    Santa strode on down the aisle,

With his funny paunch like jelly.

    And a merry, carefree smile.

As he stood before his subjects

    And looked o'er the radiant throng,

Stealing o'er us crept a feeling

    Like a bound heart's stifled song

Something gripped him, held him silent,

    And his smile was twisted now,

As he gazed out o'er the masses,

Grave, the furrows at his brow.

And a look of sincere pity

Floated outward with his sight.

As he spoke to those he treasured

There on Greystone's Holy Night.

Then he spoke, and words of wisdom

Floated out about the room,

And the tone of friendship blended

With the echoed carols' tune.

He spoke of Christmas spirit

And of blessings of the day,

Of the pleasures gained by giving,

And the joy of Yule-tide play

But not one word did he utter

Of how he had made the fight

That had gained for us the pleasure

Of this, Greystone's Holy Night.

No such word by him was spoken,

But I crouching in my chair,

Watched him, watched him, watched him,

And I saw a vision there.

I saw a staunch man fighting

For the things he knew should be,

That were needed for his patients,

    Were they ever to be free.

Through the years he'd fought and struggled

    'Gainst scoffers' jeers and chaff,

'While the hypocrites were scorning,

    And the heartless mortal laughed.

Inch by inch he fought and conquered,

Till "Behold Those Merry Lights."

HE WHO GAVE THEM was our Santa

    On that Greystone's Holy Night.

There were few of us gay patients

    Who knew just who Santa was

That 'twas he who ruled old Greystone

    With his code of mercy's laws.

And his laughter shook the wires

    Of the myriad, dancing lights.

Even they saluted Santa

    On old Greystone's Holy Night.

None guessed that funny Santa

    Just joked and laughed, because

No one had ever read about

    A grieving Santa Claus.

But I knew that he was sighing,

'Cause there was no more to do

That could make old Greystone better

For the likes of me and you.

And as I sat there and watched him,

Somehow a mighty wave

Swept to me his heart's endeavors

From the cradle to the grave.

Strength to fight for weaker humans,

Pity for those helpless heads.

You folks maybe didn't hear it,

But that's what old Santa said.

But if he could only read us

His regrets would take to flight,

For he'd know four thousand blessings

Rose on Greystone's Holy Night.

THANKS TO COMMISSIONER ELLIS

I am sitting tonight, Mr. Ellis,

In one of your great institutes.

Where health, peace and comfort are granted

And laughter to lives long mute.

Just one among thousands who faltering

In the strange garbled battle of fate,

Have come 'neath your wing for protection.

Thank God that it wasn't too late!

I didn't think I was worth saving

When I entered this haven of rest,

A burly inebriate raving

But a longing for health in my breast.

The way I've been strengthened and treated

The health and the hope I was doled

Have brought like a rainbow at sunrise

153

The glorious birth of a soul.

I can't find the words to emblazon

    The gratitude down in my heart;

A new life's been laid out before me

    By your subjects at this human mart.

But I'm writing my thanks as I'm able

    For the good that's been done, and my hand

Shall ever be raised for New Jersey,

    And for you and this refuge of man.

As you pause from the day's occupations,

    And silently gaze toward the west,

May pride bring your earl exaltation,

    As you welcome quiet night with it's rest.

As you meet the grave gaze of your daughter,

    And peer in the eyes of your son,

Man! isn't it grand they salute you

    For the merciful work you have done?

And we who have gained health and comfort

    Tho' our bodies be held between walls,

Offer our thanks to New Jersey,

    And to those who have given us our all.

On, oh you monarch of mansions,

Thru land that just mercy expends;

From the shadows smile hearts ever grateful

To Ellis, a merciful man.

ONE OF LIFE'S TRAGEDIES

Listen, world, to a crazy tale,

    Sobbed out in a maudlin way,

Of woman who traveled a fearsome trail,

    Who forgot that there was a day.

With her life all dark, from the cradle up,

    And she just a lump of clay.

Susan Young was the woman's name,

    Blithesome, and fair, and gay,

Heart as clean as an altar's flame,

    Yet she gave her soul as pay,

Pay to the sons of high toned folk,

    Who traveled the great white way.

But tho' she died in a crimson gown,

    Here's one who stood at her bier,

And on her casket, cheap and brown

    I shed an unshamed tear,

For I'd seen her soul fight for its goal

    And she won at the last, 'tis clear.

I sauntered down Baxter one morning,

    Crossed over to dark, gloomy Pell.

On the street it was quiet, but the forming

    Of opium reek cast its spell,

And I thought of the thousands within the dens,

    Who lived in that foggy hell.

When out of a joint— 'twas the house of Ling—

    A creature so strange rolled out,

That I wondered what kind of a human thing

    Could so drag itself about.

'Twas a woman, pale and ghastly-eyed,

    A dope-crazed, weaving lout.

She staggered up and with smirking leer

    She peered straight in my eyes.

And begged for the price of a yen hok steer

    As into my soul she pried,

For I saw a poem in that wretched form,

    With a heart of valued prize.

Did she want to eat? What did I mean?

    Sure! said she, when the shot

Would fill her veins with a fairy's dream,

She'd enjoy some grub, why not?

She filled the needle with steady hand,

And sighed as it hit the spot.

Then the drug stream grappled her deadened brain,

And her eyes began to shine

Away from her lips the line of pain,

As we sat us down to dine,

She told the tale of a soul's despair,

And a life thrown on the line.

She tapped my hand with a clammy claw,

And looked straight in my face.

Despite the creed of man-made laws,

I saw there a plain stamped trace

Of mother love and a guiltless heart,

Tho' she'd weakened in life's race.

She told of a home with a faithful man,

And a baby sick in her arms,

Of the lack of funds for a lengthy span,

And her darling in fever's charm,

Of a desperate man gone out to steal

To protect their home from harm.

For days and nights she fought with death

And her husband sent off to jail,

ONE OF LIFE'S TRAGEDIES

She prayed at the harsh spasmodic breath

    Of the babe, delirious, pale.

'Twas then she'd sampled a bit of dope,

    For she dared not weaken and fail.

Three months went by. The baby came

    Back from its fever and pain,

The husband died in a lousy jail

    And she with a craving brain,

For the soothing drug that had gripped her firm

    And held her bound to its train.

For the kiddie's sake she did her best,

    Worked when work could be had,

Then the panic came, and hunger pressed

    Her out where life was bad,

But food she got for her baby's need

    From the Great White Way's gay lads.

She'd raised the child, had her in school,

    And the daughter could never dream

That her mother was floating in frothy pool

    And hopeless to leave the stream

Of the underworld where the sad wrecks dwell,

    That we call just dope fiends.

Then this Susie Young, unknown, unsung,

Smiled-'twas a twisted smile,

As she took a hop needle from Ling Chung

    And poured in an awful pile.

She whispered, "At last my task is done,

    And I'm going to rest awhile."

'Twas an overdose, and the end came fast,

    Susie spoke no more

We saw her smile and breathe her last

    There on Ling Chung's floor

And a newspaper clipping in her hand

    Told of a wedding's lore.

She'd played the game till the girl had wed,

    Then she wanted to leave disgrace.

Went with a Christlike glow 'bout her head

    And His faith upon her face,

We carted her off to the potter's field,

    But she'd won in a glorious race.

Thou Art Known

I have heard about a woman

    Who has taken sincere stand

For the ill ones of the nation

    That are gripped in iron hand.

I inscribe here of a mortal

    Who helps sick ones greet the dawn,

Who stands guard at mercy's portals,

    And her name is Garrison.

* * * * *

Oh, friend, whom we know to be tested friend,

    Who aids us in our surging fight for health,

To you in salutation meek we bend,

    And gratefully our prayers send up their wealth.

We hear of you and what you oft have done

    For us, who stare from realm of chilly bars,

Our worldless thanks are rapt as beams of setting sun,

Are just as true as promise in those friendly stars.

Ah! friend, we hear that you're a gentle soul

Who for the helpless, stricken ones would toil,

We hear that in your heart there's but one goal

That deep in mercy's cause you tireless moil.

Beneath these darting spires we patients know,

By some instinct, by science undefined,

When they who come and note our saddened woe

Are touched at heart, and strengthen firing lines.

The other day as you went thru' our peaceful ward,

From room to room, 'twixt walls of somber grey,

I from the shadows saw the temper of your sword,

And knew that God had sent an angel to our fray,

I crouched down in my corner, dropped my head,

Lest you might see the blessing in my eyes

As you spoke low of "furnishings, of newer chairs and beds."

Ah, then I knew that up in Paradise

A Watching Father still had us in mind

And would not let us suffer 'twixt these walls,

That he would send more workers to our lines,

That he had heard our sighs, and marked their call.

Beyond the pale where demons of unrest

Creep and slink through thoughts untaught, untrained,

THOU ART KNOWN

For some a savage hell in bellowed chest,

    In some depressive, hopelessness of tainted brain,

Gathered here upon a hilltop much like Calvary,

    We trembling ones must pass our yearning years

As Jesus did up on that ancient, torturing tree,

    And as His friends did then, you offer sincere tears.

Like Him we're guiltless of premeditated sin,

    Like Him some of us must pass on in pain,

But when an end comes to this tinseled din,

    The guiltless must meet on that golden plain.

We're happy, many of us here, because there's such

    As you are with us hour by hour,

You and these loyal doctors fashion much

    Of good, of joy, you know not all your power.

We're well content in this, God's refuge home,

    For here quiet comfort spreads its restful vines.

We wait life's sunset and the last deep purple gloam

    When wearied minds fly on and leave disease behind.

So to you, gentle friend, who helps to steer our craft

    Across rough breakers, till the storm be done,

Keep in your mind that they who let a sad heart laugh

    Have earned their crown, and joy eternal won.

You see, oh, Mrs. Garrison, we know your thoughts,

We know our friends who bear our banners thru'.

You quietly gave your best, and to us comfort brought.

Peace, friend, we know of you, we know of you.

Author's Note:

Composed in vain attempt to portray our appreciation of Mrs. Garrison and those who work with her in the rehabilitation of humanity.

Inspired by Mrs. Garrison one day while on a tour of inspection. Dedicated with all the admiration that only a group of grateful patients can muster.

The Trail Of The Little Red Ball

I stood at a table where stakes were all high,

    And feverish humans abound;

The wheel's gaudy colors go whirling on by,

    And fortunes are changed by its rounds.

Fair women are grasping the shiny brass rail,

    And watching wealth's tide rise and fall,

Gazing half wild, face tensioned and pale,

    On the trail of the little ball.

Many thousands were lost and thousands were won

    As the little red ball went around.

For some it meant leisure, with work they were done,

    For some just a suicide's mound.

Young and old seemed enchanted, the game held them fast.

    On the wheel they would gamble their all,

And, losing, they stumbled to cognac glass,

On the trail of the little red ball.

Here a youth bets his roll on one turn of the wheel,

And with face white as death, waits the call,

Then he mutters a curse and despondent he reels

From the reek of the crowded hall.

So is it true of most of the world,

We gamble things dearest of all,

And losing, give up, and banners we furl,

On the trail of the little red ball.

A Tale Of Long Ago

There's a grave up in Alaska

    Where the gruesome Yukon's sweeping

With a crooked wooden cross stuck at its head.

    Archie lies near Athabasca,

On a snow-capped mountain sleeping,

    Forgotten save by one who mourns his dead.

Just a gawky cowpunch brother

    With a homely face of honor,

And an honest eye that wouldn't see despair.

    Like him I shall find no other;

But for him I'd been a goner,

    The kid who stuck thru' weather foul or fair.

When our mother died, stark sorrow

    Seemed to fill the ranch's corners,

And her gentle voice seemed calling from each stone.

    "Arch" and I faced drear to-morrows.

So we quit the house of mourners.

    Sold out the herds and hit the trail alone.

"Arch" was scarce a man-just twenty,

    But he'd bucked the cattle ranges,

And could draw a gat as quick as lightning's flash.

    We'd both learned 'bout life a plenty,

Things taught by the border's changes,

    We could even throw together breakfast hash.

"Arch" was always quiet and steady,

    He did a lot of thinking,

With a woman, dog or horse he was an ace,

    And he was always ready

When hope and peace were sinking

    To give you all his strength to win your race.

I have seen him rope a stallion

    With the hate for mankind blazing

Out of red-rimmed eyes, arid conquer fairly, too,

    And I've seen that wild horse wither,

Without any brutal hazing,

    Tho' "Arch" was smiling, he was bleeding, too.

But I'm getting from my story.

    And I'll hustle up and shout it:

We hit the dust to try Alaska's mines,

A TALE OF LONG AGO

There was gold enough, great glory!

But when you went to get it,

    You couldn't in a week dig out a dime.

We didn't have much money,

    Just thought we wouldn't need it.

We kept our ranch and thanked our stars for that!

    Life didn't give much honey.

Hard luck, we didn't heed it,

    But we tried to grin, tho' both were nearly flat.

One day we heard a rumor

    That a new rich field had opened,

And we hit the trail for Fairbanks right away.

    With the sourdoughs and boomers

We rushed on yet scarcely hoping

    That we'd ever dig out gold from yellow clay.

We got parted from the others,

    And our dog team kept us busy,

So before we knew it we were badly lost.

    That stark silence, how it smothered

Us, and made us fairly dizzy,

    As we tried to brush our eyelids free from frost.

Three days out, the ague got me

    And the kid just wrapped and bundled

Me up tight and tied me to the blooming sleigh,

    I faded right out of the picture,

And "Arch" must just have trundled

    The whole caboose across the frozen ways.

Sixteen days he toiled and suffered,

    Just to save my worthless carcass,

When he could have left me there and saved his skin,

    But he ate the dogs, the duffer

Knew that Fate would right soon mark us,

    And he froze off both his hands to get me in

He crept into Nome one morning

    With his arms just limp and flopping,

And mumbled to the priest that I was sick,

    When reason came adorning,

I heard his breathing, chopping.

    He grinned and gasped, "I'm going. Good-bye, Dick."

Oh, it's hell to give a brother

    To the sullen grave of darkness,

When he's all you have to make you think of home.

    You feel like you'd really rather

Face yourself the clammy starkness

    Than in lonely misery o'er the wild world roam.

There's a grave up in Alaska

Where a brave lad's quietly sleeping

And I made the cross and placed it at his head;

Now I'm far from Athabasca,

Twixt grey walls, and hope is seeping,

And lucky "Arch" rests with the martyred dead.

LIFE

"What is Life?" I asked the stars
    As I sat alone one night,
Sat and gazed thru the grating bars
    And they twinkled their answer "Light."
"What is life?" I asked ·the sky
    As I stared toward the arch above.
And the answer came on a zephyr's sigh,
    "Life is only love."
"What is life?" I asked the moon,
    That hung like a silvery boat.
And the answer came from a cliff-perched loon
    "Life is an unknown note."
And a chorus lifted its lilting chimes
    Up on the breeze to me.
"Life if you make it will always shine
    Or be dark as you cause it to be."

LOVE'S MEMORY

Woman thou art, and yet to me much more.

    To morning sunbeams' silvery spirit art thou kin,

Within thy smile a world of cheer in store

    Sends out its wave to show the joy within.

Proud thy queenly, placid brow, with closely fondling mist

    Of silk as soft as tuft of fairy's curls.

Back through the ages some relations on the list,

    That boast of royal blood from other worlds.

Ah! sweet spirit with thy glad incessant laugh,

    Thou nurse who gowned as lily of the lake,

Thy soul is match to color that is half

    The fight, for we who of thy doctrine shall partake.

Yet when you speak, the song within your voice

    Awakes regret within a heart where grief repines

That I could not have long before dwelt in, rejoiced,

    In rapture that now fills this heart of mine.

So sordid, drab my days, before you flitted in

    So dull the sun, so dim the watchful stars.

For me just unrest, loneliness and sullen sin,

    Then, God! I had to meet you back of madhouse bars.

Soon we shall part, once more I go to tread

    The unblazed trails that twist, and curve, and wind,

But with a vision now to grant my hungry soul good bread.

    A sweet soul's memory, tho' she be left behind.

You nor the world shall ever guess or know

    That I've met love and bid that love begone.

You with your heart and hair of glistening snow

    May yet smile on me in that refuge up, beyond.

THE FOOL

I vowed I would have my way

    And scorned the old man's rules,

But long ere the end I paid.

    Oh! I was a fool-a fool,

I drank when the wine was red

    And glutted my wild desires,

I laughed when the old sage said

    I was playing, with dangerous fire.

I toyed with the erring crew

    Who laugh at clean health's rules,

Ah God! had I only known,

    But I was a fool-a fool!

Neath the lights of sensual red

    I threw the best of my youth,

Proud held my modern head,

    And mocked at the sages' truth,

I dabbled in things condemned,

In the end 'twas a costly school,

But youth never comprehends,

　　And I was a fool-a fool!

I married and settled down

　　With a blue-eyed pal so true,

O'er the past raised a mighty mound,

　　Nor dreamed that the past I'd rue.

So happy, so gloriously glad,

　　Were we in our comfy home,

Nor dreamed we would ever be sad.

　　Nor listened to conscience's groan.

Complacent I cast away

　　All thought of the bygone tools,

I didn't know I'd have to pay,

　　For I was a fool-a fool!

For a babe was given our home.

　　And my wife divinely had smiled,

Then died with heart-rending moan,

　　And I started to pay for life's wiles.

For the babe was crippled and blind.

　　Shapeless as heel-crushed jewel,

The past came back to my mind,

　　Ah, I was a fool-a fool!

Lifters Of The Veil

Out of the warming light
   Into the dim dumb haze,
Away from lights once bright,
   Deep in the foggy maze.
Souls of mankind laugh,
   Spirits of humans wail.
Gathered in masses the chaff
   Waiting the rise of the veil.
Spectres that grope through the dusk,
   Shadows that merge with the past,
Bodies with only the husk
   Of joys too precious to last.
Protected, close guarded, detained,
   Unfaithful our feet to the trail.
Shrouded the eyes of the brain,
   Now awaiting the rise of the veil.
Medicos: princes of peace,

Strive with a sincere belief

That darkness be lessened and cease,

That wrecks may be saved from the reef.

Awaiting a new wisdom's spawn,

Struggling in murky gale,

Awaiting the glimmer of dawn

And the rise of the lilac veil.

Tireless our doctors toil,

Staunch in their merciful works,

Bearing continuous moil,

To straighten out mental quirks.

Unsung, unhallowed they dwell

In this manse, that health may prevail,

To lighten our seething hell,

To lift up the purple veil.

Eureka, we sing in refrain.

New health you have found for man,

Found rest for the tainted brain,

And sent great joy o'er the land.

Peace thou hast spread o'er the sod

And straightened God's favorite trails.

May you receive peace from God,

Thou lifters of blinding veils.

A Little Kiddie Waiting For Her Dad On Number Four

I was rubbing wax upon the floor

Of our reception hall,

Humming to keep up my spirits

'Twixt old Greystone's mocking walls.

When I saw a youngster standing,

Posing there before the door.

Just a little kiddie waiting

For her Dad on Number Four.

There she stood in childish glory

With a smile upon her face

Like unto the fair Madonna

With her sacred quiet grace.

In a chair the mother huddled

And her worn hands gripped the rounds.

Pain and sorrow, grief and misery

On her countenance I found.

Just a loyal, faded woman

Sitting silent by the door,

Just a faithful life-mate waiting

For her man on Number Four.

The youngster's chubby fingers

Tightly clutched a paper poke

And she smiled and lisped so quaintly;

"I have brought my Dad some smokes."

Something in the picture gripped me

As I shoved the block along

And a wave of glad elation

Brought my heart a long-lost song.

For I too had someone waiting,

Where the western breezes play,

Where the sunset paints its glory

O'er two little grassy graves.

Some day 'twixt those mounds I'll

     slumber,

And find rest forevermore

With two little tots that's waiting

For their Dad of Number Four.

CHRISTMAS AT GREYSTONE PARK

Hear 'em buddy, hear 'em,

    Golly ain't it fine

To hear those church bells ringin'

    Out at Christmas time?

Everybody happy,

    Candles everywhere,

Stars of gold and silver

    Dancin' in the air.

Everybody's laughin',

    Presents all around

Radio is bustin' with

    Sousa, I'll be bound.

Doctors workin', hurryin',

    Not a sigh nor groan,

Chucklin' about the kiddies

With their toys at home.

Nurses cut off corners

    Hummin' mighty gay,

Don't you wish that Christmas

    Happened every day?

Wish I knew that everyone

    Was havin' eats and fun

Like us lucky patients

    Here on old Three-One.

Let's forget our troubles

    And listen to the bells,

By this time next Christmas

    We all may be well.

So come on buddy, shake 'em,

    And sing a song or two,

With things like this a goin'

    A body can't be blue.

The table's loaded heavy

    The cake and fruit are fine,

So come on pards and join us

    While the village church bells chime.

Just A Rhyming Raver
On North-Three-One

Sittin' by the window

As the sun sinks low,

Starin' thru' the grating

At the purple-crimson glow.

Just one of the patients

Whose race is nearly run,

Just a rhyming raver

On North-Three-One.

Life has lost its glamor.

I've sampled everything.

Drank of gall and nectar,

Learned to cry and sing.

Tired of working puzzles,

Wearied of the fun,

Just a rhyming raver,

On North-Three-One.

All the world seems empty,

My loved ones laid away,

Joints are gone rheumatic,

My hair is gettin' grey.

Wonder what is waitin'

On the shore of chosen ones?

Will they take a rhyming raver

From North-Three-One?

Will I still be an outcast

For aye misunderstood?

Shall I build another castle

On a base of rotted wood?

Will I get a work-parole

Up there above the sun?

Will the Staff believe a raver

From North-Three-One?

But there ain't no use in sighin'

Cause things ain't breakin' right,

So I'll just cut out the pinin'

And laugh away my fright.

Workin' 'mongst the flowers

With the greenhouse gang,

JUST A RHYMING RAVER ON NORTH-THREE-ONE

Good grub, a bed to sleep in,

So I don't care a hang.

Playin' pool of evenings

And our radio

Always soothin', cheerin'

Good as any show.

Attendants not too cranky

Supervisors square,

Doctors always ready

When you need their care.

So my rhymes from now on

Shall be full of fun,

'Cause I'm just a rhymin' raver

On North-Three-One.

OBSESSIONAL

I was staring through the grating,

    Like a convict, death awaiting,

Sat with sad heart palpitating

    In a manse of mumbling men.

When a cold hand grasped my shoulder,

    Like a demon growing bolder,

Midnight growing cold and colder,

    I could not move again;

And a gripping, helpless, feeling,

    Held me thrall within its trend.

"What," I pondered, "is this feeling,"

    That o'er my tired heart's stealing,

Setting my poor brain a reeling

    Like a tortured soul in pain?

Is it ghost of past unfettered

    That had followed me to hector,

Hopes and dreams that I have shattered,

    Come to sear my puzzled brain?

If so, ghost, have mercy on me.

    Ghost, I beg you to refrain.

Then there came a rasping sighing,

    Like a beauteous maid, who, dying,

Begs of God to let her linger

    In this vale, though full of tears;

And a hollow labored moaning,

    Like a wounded warrior groaning,

Like a mother bidding good-by

    To her first-born babe so dear.

A nameless, pleading, sobbing,

    Ghastly in this manse of fear.

Then there came a muttered whining,

    Like a death trapped creature pining,

And a gurgling, choking horror,

    Seemed to freeze my very blood;

Like a glacier's wind, low sweeping,

    Came that weird hysteric weeping,

And remorse, embittered reaping

    Absorbed me like a flood;

With a slimy, crawling, gushing

Torrent flow of bloody mud.

"Stop, oh stop" I cried, "This madness.

Cease this chilly, racking sadness,

Let me get myself together,

Ere you shatter my poor mind."

And the ghost rasped out, "Cease whining,

For. for you, there's much repining,

You have soused in poison liquor,

While good deeds you've cast behind."

And the hidden ghost now chortled

Like a herd of dying swine.

Then the ghostly voice grew quieter

Seeming less, and less the blighter,

Like a heaven-inspired writer

Who has viewed a vision clear,

And in tones now calm and level

I was told just how the devil

Had embalmed me, cursed me, left me

Sodden with all creature's jeers.

Hence this real reincarnation,

In the manse of groundless fears.

And as midnight struck, the spirit

Rustled, and the draft so near it

OBSESSIONAL

Slammed the doors, and rattled windows.

    Lo! I found myself alone.

Just one word had marked its going,

    A long drawn echo flowing

On faint, night-zephyr blowing.

    Came the whispered word "Atone",

Like a master leaves a pupil

    With a lesson carved in stone.

Then I turned from that cold grating,

    No longer death awaiting,

With my thoughts composed toward mating

    With reason, and with health,

And I laughed aloud, "Oh Spectre

    That I thought had come to hector,

I shall bide the rules at Greystone

    And absorb its gloried wealth.

Like a lily draws the dewdrops

    From nature's verdant pelt."

I'm Telling The World
That I'm One

What is that place 'mongst the maples,

    UP there on that proud rearing hill?

That's where, when health's lost its staples,

    A body is purged of its ills.

Yes, that is where I'm now living,

    But you see, I'm on ground parole,

If you wish, a treat I'll be giving,

    A tale of this refuge of souls.

No, I'm not very sick it is true, Sir,

    I've been here since August you know,

'Tis a wonder I ever came through, Sir,

    And the credit, to Greystone must go.

You say that it looks like a prison?

    Why stranger you must be in fun,

That's a refuge where souls have arisen,

I'M TELLING THE WORLD THAT I'M ONE

And I'm telling the world that I'm one.

I wish I could show all the people,

    Who have such awe, fear and dread,

How different things are 'neath these steeples,

    And the treatments by psychiatrists spread.

There are mortals who owe all their treasures

    To the great, grey haven's green slopes,

Where they've studied their souls, and been measured

    By God for a new lease on hope.

There're thousands who owe Greystone plaudits

    Because of a great race well run,

There're some who eternally laud it,

    And I'm telling the world that I'm one.

The peace and the quiet about you,

    The health that responds to your call,

The beauty of nature that routs you.

    Man! There is joy in it all.

The triumph, the wonder, the glory,

    Of seeing a new life unfold,

Rehearsing God's old placid story,

    Of mercy Samaritans extolled.

The smiles, as a tired brain is strengthened,

    As a mind blossoms out in the sun,

There are many who've had lifetimes lengthened,

    And I'm telling the world that I'm one.

The system in science's chapel,

    The magic of dentistry's chair,

The flash of a skilled surgeon's scalpel

    Work in quiet harmony there.

From the arch of the modern Reception

    To the rambling Dorm on the hill,

The glow of sound health's reflection

    Is blended with consummate will.

'Tis no fun to be only half living,

    To limp through a life scarce begun,

There're sortie who've craved therapy's giving,

    And I'm telling the world that I'm one.

I came in a panic and flurry,

    My mind was a sorrowful mess,

I had lived in too much of a hurry

    And was pretty far gone, I confess.

I raved, so they say, without pausing,

    It seemed that my hour had come,

For years my neglect had been causing

    The debt, that had mounted up some.

I trembled and shook-darned good reason—

I'M TELLING THE WORLD THAT I'M ONE

Till the medicos got into swing,

Then came convalescent season,

And I started to climb in the ring.

I have cursed, when the silence seemed screaming

In the starkness of night, when the bars

Mocked me, with cold, steely meaning,

Alone with the night, and the stars.

My every breath was a plea for death,

Life seemed but a witless pun,

But there're many folks saved from an early grave,

And I'm telling the world that I'm one.

I faced my soul as the scenes unrolled,

Plain came the truth to me,

I saw for myself the wreck unfold,

And the man that I used to be.

I saw the past, and a judgment sword

Hung, as I gasped for breath,

As I screamed at spectres in the dark,

And searched for the trail blazed "Death".

With a face all hair and a hopeless stare,

I saw what the locust had done,

As I faced my Lord, in that mental ward,

In the halls of North-Three-One.

But the doctors fought thru' the wint'ry days,

    And before the winter was done,

A group of minds had pierced their haze,

    And I'm telling the world that I'm one,

That's all of my story, Stranger,

    Greystone made a "come back" of me,

You can read my rhymes in the "Psychogram"

    Neath the heading R. D. C.

Tell all you meet of the wonders

    That in old Greystone are done,

Where many have shook off life's blunders,

    And I'm telling the world that I'm One.

MEMOIRS OF THE DAWN

Sometimes, in my hour of reflection,

    As I wander 'twixt Greystone's high

        walls,

I drift into deep retrospection

    And, God! I get tired of it all.

Without one true comrade to mourn me,

    When I drift o'er the sunset trail,

Not even a dog's howl to scorn me,

    Just chaff 'neath relentless flail.

It seems that I never knew friendship

    Since I wandered away from the range.

I'd grown up in a Montana saddle.

    The Lord only knows why I changed.

Somehow, back there life is sweeter.

    I can't just put it in words,

But you feel clean and care-free and reck less

Like the rollicking calves of the herd.

At sunrise you lope o'er the mesa

    With dew on the neck of the roan,

Singing a half tuneless ditty,

    You and your broncho alone.

At night when the cattle are resting

    You lazily stare at the stars,

Little dreaming the treach'ry of Venus,

    Little knowing the bloodshed of Mars.

Where 'the whippoorwill calls from the

        canyon,

    And you hear the weird hoot of an owl,

While out on the buttes of the bad-lands

    The lone coyotes mournfully howl.

That's where I learned of life's lessons,

    That to conquer you had to be brave,

That a promise once made was as sacred

    As a prayer at a mother's grave.

That's where I first knew true friendship,

    In the days of the six-gun law,

And I learned to reverence virtue

    From a pock-marked. Osage squaw.

'Tis a long, long trail to the prairies,

To the spread of the old Bar T,

Which I've owned since I was a stripling,

Before rum got the better of me.

The Osage tribe then was friendly,

And a band corraled up on my range

To doctor a few of their ponies

Which were sick with a kind of a mange.

One day I met one of the women

With eyes like a dewdrop at dawn.

Her friendship grew into a treasure,

The girl-squaw, Sleeping Fawn.

The months sped on, and still they camped

Beside my branding lanes.

And Sleeping Fawn and I would ride

Together o'er the plains.

She taught me everything of good,

She made me understand

That honor was a thing of gold

And virtue God's demand.

She told me somewhere I would meet

A white girl of my race

Who'd bring much light into my heart

And glorify my face.

197

But something, oh! so wistful,

    In that little squaw-girl's tone

Bade me look deep into her eyes

    There I saw her soul alone.

But when I tried to draw her close,

    Two hopeless tears were drawn

From out the velvet azure

    Of the eyes of Sleeping Fawn.

"No, big-boy Dick, we no can go

    Against the white man's law.

You have mines, an' big, big ranch;

    Me, I'm just a squaw."

"You are a white man rancher's boy.

    Your friends no speak with me.

A blooded pacer you will ride,

    And me a mustang breed."

"But every morning when you wake,

    Just smile big, at the dawn,

And I will always do the same."

    So whispered Sleeping Fawn.

There was no cheapened, trifling kiss,

    As we stood on life's cliff.

If I'd have kissed her we'd have wed,

But, ah! that little *if.*

Just then there came unto my ears

A rumble that I knew

Came from ten thousand pounding hoofs

As o'er the plains they flew.

I wheeled my cayuse toward the girl,

And grasped her in my fright.

I swung her to my saddle,

And we leaped into the night.

"Make it, Devil, make it,

Or we've all three got to die

Devil boy, you've got to win."

And how that brooch did try.

"Listen, Fawn," I panted,

As Devil found his stride.

"We're heading for the river.

It's the only trail to ride."

She gently pressed my shoulder

While nearer death was drawn,

And what a death beneath these hoofs

For little Sleeping Fawn.

Behind us thundered on the herd

Ten thousand steers or more

Were plunging wild in scared stampede,

    With horns that longed to gore.

Just then a crash, and darkness came.

    When I knew life again

The herd was gone; 'neath something soft

    I lay upon the plains.

I rolled aside, the soft thing lay

    A little form in pawn.

Dead! dead! and, oh! so crushed and beat,

    My little Sleeping Fawn.

She'd thrown her body over mine,

    To save me from the herd.

She'd given her gentle life for mine,

    And left without a word.

Those are the friendships that we have

    Out where the wind is free.

I found my gold,—she said I would—,

    Out on the old Bar T.

And when the other patients sleep

    I wake to greet the dawn.

The quiet peace that's granted me

    Is the smile of Sleeping Fawn.

The Passing Of A Rose

A man once plucked a flower,

    Tore it away from its place

From the arch of its mother bower,

    And gazed at its beauty and grace.

Drank in its glorious trust,

    Basked in the radiance there,

Then cast it down in the dust,

    Because it was no more fair.

Crushed it beneath his foot,

    Nor mentioned its death in his talk.

But a life had passed 'neath his boot

    And bled on the garden walk.

The man won a girl's sweet trust

    And coaxed her away from home.

In a year she was in the dust,

    And the boot to crush her was prone,

The rose bloom gone from her cheek,

    The azure gone from her eye.

She, broken, disgraced and meek,

    Died as the flower died.

She wavered and cried her pain,

    But the heart of the man was cold,

And the tale of the flower slain

    And crushed was once more told.

TO MARCIA

Many joys are held in store,

And for you they shine galore,

Romping, laughing, merry, gay,

Calling birdies on the way.

I just know you're bound to meet

A fairy band to fondly greet.

Carry on, oh, dainty maid,

Under maples' gentle shade

Run and sing, send echos free,

Romp, and tell the world your glee.

You are of God's favorite tree.

Author's Note:

Composed about Master Jack McMurray upon hearing of the dexterity with which he handled a sailing vessel, the performance of which would have done credit to one twice his years.

The thought implied was that his life as now might always bear standards as clear as the white sails on the craft he handled.

Presented with the sincere regards of the author.

Cap O' The Sail Patrol

He flung to the breeze his snowy sails,

    Swung sharp is boat around,

Hand on tiller he crouched by the rail,

    For the waters in reefs abound.

He lifted his boyish face to the sky,

    His laugh scorned the hidden reef.

He jibbed his canvas and passed on by

    The unseen, dangerous grief.

Only a lad but a brawny lad,

    His eyes with a careful gleam,

A steady hand and a smile so glad

    It shone like a prince's sheen.

Over the waves he sent his craft,

    Lined out straight for the goal,

And his father mused in quiet content

    With Cap O' the Sail Patrol.

Sail on, oh Jack though the way be rough,

And breakers would drive you away.

Stick to the helm, and do your stuff

As you have started in work and play.

May you ever command clean, snowy sails,

As you skipper your own patrol.

May you smile as now, at the harried gales,

The captain of your soul.

Hold your bow to the compass point,

Steer straight to the glorious goal.

Nor waver at breaking tops'l joint

Oh Cap O' the sail patrol.

Though patched and torn, keep white your sail

As your father has always done.

Son of a noble in laughter or wails

A captain in work or fun.

May your craft glide in to the harbor's plank

As gay as she left for her goal.

May you sign with pride on the Master's blank

Oh Cap O' The Sail Patrol.

Author's Note:

The thought of a student nurse leaving all influences of her home to train for nursing amongst strangers in a strange land granted the inspiration for this work.

Who knows, perhaps, before some faithful hearted girl, lonely and tempted, may dress for a party perchance her eyes might sweep about her room ere she leaves and some train of thought gained from my crude rhyme might help the party turn out differently than it otherwise would? And if so, trebly am I repaid.

A FATHER SPEAKS

And so, my girls, you're going to the City,

    To brave the world and learn to be a nurse.

You're going where there's mighty little pity

    For one who ever carries empty purse.

And as I've taught your baby feet to bear you

    O'er smooth, clean trails away from jagged stones,

I offer this, that ignorance can't ensnare you

    When you are out there in the world alone.

This great career that is one of your choosing

    Is one that merits well in God's grave eyes.

Because of you a life may yet, while losing

    Its mortal flight, sail on to Paradise.

Watch well your compass, through the trip of training;

    Keep pride in hand, nor should you play too much.

You'll meet rebuffs, but meet them uncomplaining,

    And with the internes have but business touch.

Remember, girls, that tests are all about you,

    And watch for coyote smiles around life's bends.

Think not of nightly frolics, for they'll rout you;

    Dance programmes with your charts will never blend.

Though you have to scrub a floor or wash a railing;

    You'll get a month of that, you well can bet,

Don't go at it with sulks nor useless wailing,

    Just tackle it and grin out through the sweat.

Just keep those quiet smiles of yours a-flashing

    When you fix a pain-racked, feverish patient's bed,

And speak a cheery word, though hopes be crashing.

    For the sick ones don't forget what nurse has said.

Keep to yourself when shallow mortals gather

    Nor sink to shallow ways to win a friend,

Lest you be judged as birds of that same feather.

    Alpha starts: Omega is the end.

And keep the sister comradeship a-burning,

    Each guard the other, for each understands.

The moral code of man is often luring,

    And shame is often laughed at in the land.

We're glad we're here at home to get your letters,

    And hope for one that reads you've won your goal,

With black-lined cap and free of student's fetters,

A FATHER SPEAKS

In mercy's army, captain of your souls.

If things go wrong, the old home's always ready,

And ma and I will be there at the gate

To welcome you; and her old eyes are steady,

We'll watch the home trail; at its end we'll wait.

We hope that all through life each flying minute

Will have for you just sixty ticks of good,

That you may gorge success and joy within it,

And blossom out in glorious sisterhood.

And if you'll carry virtue's jeweled banner

Throughout the fight until your cross is won,

There's not a saint can boast a blessing grander,

And God shall say, "Oh, gentle nurse, well done."

When glad vacation time is drawing nearer,

Come home, where rest and peace reign quiet and still.

Just idle 'long the path that's ever dearer,

That leads to home amongst verdant hills.

SONG OF THE BARS

There's a chill in the air and a moan in the hall,

There's a cry of despair and grief 'twixt the walls,

There's a curse and a blessing that rise to the stars,

As we mortals keep guessing the song of the bars.

Oh, the bars, those bars, those rusty, taunting bars,

They choke me and they've broke me,

Those silent, mocking bars.

Here a soul begs to die, and another would dwell

Down here 'neath blue skies, and another craves hell,

Mumbling and gurgling, as dementia jars,

All trying to learn that weird song of the bars.

Ah, the bars, cold bars, those hideous, leering bars,

They taunt me and they flaunt me,

Those soul accusing bars.

They are kind to us here, or we'd falter and fall,

But there's merciful cheer 'twixt Greystone's grey walls.

And many glad hearts have wandered afar,

Strong, well, they depart from the song of the bars.

Ah, the bars, those bars, those life protecting bars,

Their misery's drawn with flash of dawn,

Those silent, guarding bars.

Author's Note:

Composed as a testimonial for faithful, conscientious service to patients, and fairness to fellow employees which has ever characterized Peter Fitzpatrick, in charge of all the bookbinding and ruling in our Print Shop. Offered with the best wishes of the author.

Salutation To A Brother's Keeper

Faithful, sincere, have you done your bit

    Nor faltered when doubled was your load.

Toiled on nor made a grand display of it

    But kept your thoughts and feet on duty's road.

Grown old in service, for the ailing brotherhood

    Who, ill and shaken, still would do some task

To help regain their health and for their good,

    Drive out the thoughts that form a leering mask.

Grown old in helping weaker, stumbling men

    To prolong life, to quiet unruly nerves,

To boost them, aid them on and on again

    With soothing words around life's myriad curves.

I've watched you from my railed-in office space

    As you talked low and smoothed an angry one.

I've read the brother's message on your face

SALUTATION TO A BROTHER'S KEEPER

As quiet the patient grew e're you were done.

Within that shop a garden you have built,

Whose spirit e'er shall live; such deeds don't die.

The plants you started shall not fade nor wilt

Though many years and centuries pass them by.

Little did you know that oft I've seen

You as you'd take a trembling patient's arm

And guide his seared thoughts to where the gleam

Of peaceful sunshine drove out all alarm.

Across the field, charge on—Watch out, a mine is there.

A few more battles and you'll win your valor cross.

A few more buddies saved—steady, watch that flare—

And you can say that you have nothing lost.

And when at last your books are trimmed and bound

And that Supreme Collector of all human lines

0.K's your task, then, Peter, your reward is found,

And God will give you golden books to bind.

Just Coo – Coo

Me and Dick wuz buddies,

But Dick wuz kinda coo-coo.

You didn't notice it any

When he wuz workin',

But in the morning 'fore daylight,

As we wuz headin' for the round-up,

Or on the higher ridges,

Lookin' for strays,

He would get kinda dreamy lookin',

And gazin' at the dawn breakin'

In the east, he'd say

Somethin' 'bout "chariots o' the day",

With purple beacons,

And a comet striking a planet

Of rainbows that fell in

A great flower garden and

JUST COO – COO

The flash wuz the rainbows

And the flowers showing 'gainst the sky.

Yep, just kinda coo-coo.

The boulders 'long the trail he'd

Call "guards of the sacred passes

In their sombre robes of duty,"

Yep, he wuz awful coo-coo that way.

When a meadow lark piped up

He would mumble, sorta low, "One of

      Nature's

Musicians trying out its first notes."

He sed the clouds were "galleons of

Departed spirits flyin' in mass to

Their reward eternal,"

Yep, he shore was awful coo-coo.

Last fall he wandered away from the

      ranch,

Sayin' he wuz goin "to give his visions

To the groping minds of humanity," he

      rode off

Toward Great Bend, starin' at the sky

      plumb foolish.

Now I hear he's written

A lot o' poetry

And is publishin'

A whole book.

It's shore plumb sorrowful.

He wuz a top-hand buckaroo, too,

'Fore he got bit by that darned rhymin'

    bug,

Yes, sir, he's just coo-coo entire.

VERILIY, YOU SHALL FIND PEACE

Would you find peace, oh! worried soul,

    That sees no gladsome light?

Would you be free of clouds that roll

    Across your groping sight?

Would you find joy, oh! wearied heart,

    For which you constant long?

Would you bid all your grief depart,

    And list to joyous songs?

Then go, I pray, to cheerless cots

    Where there're no laughs nor joy,

And bring a smile to helpless tots,

    To sorrowed girl or boy.

Grant them a moment joyful spent,

    And to your fettered soul

A glorious wave of sweet content

Will be a sacred toll.

Those broken, aching little forms

    Are very dear to Him

Who bids the sun arise each morn

    And stars to give their glim.

Go out, I urge you, would you find

    The peaceful joy you crave,

To havens of the sick and blind.

    And make yourself a slave.

A slave to helpless, suffering ones

    Who lie in pain-racked gloom,

And long before your first day's done

    Your heart will find its boon.

For he who brings joy for awhile

    To suffering tousled head,

To God will waft a blessed smile.

    "They're favored," He hath said.

Good Advice

"Here, go and eat," the gambler said.

And flipped out a buck or two

To the gawky guy who had gone unfed,

And was starved for a ten-cent stew.

"Go on back home," the harpy said

To the green young runaway,

"You'll sweat real blood in a dress of red,

You'll pay in the end, you'll pay."

"Lead virtuous lives," the matron famed

Spoke long at a social meet,

Then hied herself to a pinochle game,

And did her best to cheat.

"Be straight, my son," the father said,

As he left for a week in town,

Then he and the gang raised glorious Ned,

And the son thought, "Dad's a clown."

"Be pure, dear," the mother said,

"And don't stay out too late."

Then she drained her glass and rolled to

bed,

And the girl was left to Fate.

THE MASCOT OF GREYSTONE PARK

"Jiggs," the fellows call him,

    Where he came from, goodness knows,

He has no famous pedigree

    And bears a homely pose.

His only vice is porterhouse

    With candy on the side.

And when a friend calls out his name

    His body twists with pride.

But if you are not on his list

    He'll leave with stately tread,

For social chats he has no time,

    He sniffs and cuts you dead.

He always seems to know his place,

    He's never in a fray,

And passes on with royal gait

Along the right of way.

There's a lot of human beings

Could clear away some fog,

If they'd take a course of lessons

From "Jiggs," our Greystone dog.

He's just a little spotted mutt,

But—say, he's mighty wise,

And what a world of friendliness

Shines from his great brown eyes.

He seems to know your feelings

When you want to play around,

Or when its time to snuggle close

Beside you on the ground.

He never does much barking.

In fact, he's dignified,

Unless some suicidal cat

Steps out to test his stride.

He wouldn't win a ribboned prize,

And he's got an awkward jog;

But he has personality,

This "Jiggs," our Greystone dog,

THE DOCTOR'S PRAYER

Lord of the great vast Heavens.

    We ask Thee to hear our prayer,

Unvarnished, uncouth, unleavened,

    But the plea of our hearts is there.

Not for ourselves are we pleading

    We dwell with the common good,

But for sick ones our souls are bleeding,

    For our sister and brotherhood.

Oh, Lord, Thou knowest our fighting

    Is true and staunch to the core,

But sickness the world is blighting.

    Help, Lord, or we sink once more,

Illness that grips the masses

    Brings dementia in its train,

The rich and the poor from life's passes

    Swarm in with staggering brains.

For them, Oh, just God, in Thy judging,

    Show us still better ways

To stay the pestilent smudging

    Of lives that ought to be gay.

Grant to us yet greater knowledge,

    That we may lighten their load.

Give strength to psychiatric college,

    That wandering feet find their road.

Help our patients to know we're striving

    To boost them on over the hills,

That our minds are ever contriving

    Some way to cure their ills.

Thanks, Lord, for the sincere brotherhood,

    For the blessings Thou gav'st in the past,

So well our pleas Thou understood

    We know Thou art near to the last.

We thank Thee, Lord, for the power

    Lent, as we groped thru' the fens,

That let us give health as a dower.

    Help us, we ask, "Amen."

LEAVING IT UP TO YOU

"How do I feel this morning?"

　　Why, I am all O-K.

Since I have started working,

　　Things ain't near so grey.

I haven't time for brooding,

　　And the hours seem but few.

I am doing the bit you set, "Doc"—

　　And I'm leaving the rest to you.

There's something 'bout this working

　　That brings peace to my mind.

It draws the good thoughts closer;

　　The drear ones slink behind.

So I'm doing the job you gave me,

　　And you bet it's helping me, too;

So I'm leaving the rest to you, "Doc"—

　　I'm leaving the rest to you.

You know when I am loafing,

225

The blues float round my head,

I don't see light nor gladness,

    And there comes the crushing dread.

Then I just fly in to working

    And laugh at the vanishing blues;

I'm leaving the rest to you, "Doc"—

    I'm leaving the rest to you.

"Do I want to leave old Greystone?"

    Well, "Doc," I'm not so sure

That I'm in an awful hurry

    Till certain that I'm cured.

For I'm getting on so fine

    I want to see it thru';

So I'm leaving it up to you, "Doc"—

    I'm leaving it up to you.

When I leave here I want to be

    Sure that I am well,

And if I went away too soon

    I might fall in a spell.

So I'll just keep on a plugging

    Till the staff votes "good as new;"

And I'm leaving the rest to you, " Doc"—

    I'm leaving the rest to you.

THAT LI'L FORGET-ME-NOT

I come to fix dis newa grave,

    An' leave da leetla pot,

With a pretty nica flower

    You a call Forget-me-not.

Are you da Mista Sexton

    Who keepa clean da grave?

I lika paya you to clean

    The one where Tony lays.

My Tony was a gooda boy,

    He learna fine in school;

He noa make da fonny face

    Nor breaka of da rule.

He win a prize in ritmatic—

    Disa plant in earthen pot,

Sooch nica friendly flower,

    You a call Forget-me-not.

Da leetla flower my Tony love,

    He tenda it each day.

He feex da eart' an' water it,

    Before he go an play.

He usa say it coulda smile,

    An' he pet da leetla pot

Where da pretty flower bloomed

    Da nica Forget-me-not.

My husban' he get kill one day

    While blasta out da stone,

An' me an' Tony isa lef'

    To liva dere alone.

I gota vera gooda job,

    A-scrubbin' office stair,

An' after school my Tony

    Woulda help a me up there.

But onea day he didn' come,

    I waita long for him,

An' then a bi a p'liceman

    Some bada message bring.

He say my leeda Tony

    Was hurta in da head,

An' pretty queek I finda out

Da leetla keed was dead.

I go in to his bed room,

    I kneela on da spot,

Da leetla plant close in my arms,

    His li'l Forget-me-not.

I crya mooch an' saya prayer

    For Tony, ah! so still,

We laya heem in nica box,

    An' take heem up da hill.

An' now each Sunday I a come

    To feex da leetla pot,

With Tony's smiling flower,

    Da nica Forget-me-not.

Now springa time is all around

    Da earth is oh so gay,

Jus' like when Tony was at home,

    When in da woods he played.

But not a one of outdoor things,

    As nica as da pot

With da leetla, smiling blossom,

    You a call Forget-me-not.

And pleasa, Mista Sexton man,

    You keepa clean da grave,

I paya you for ever' week.

    Taka care where Tony lays.

And helpa me Mista Sexton,

    Watch for da leetla pot,

With Tony's pretty flower

    You a call Forget-me-not.

ONE OF OUR GIRLS

I watched her there at the little desk,

    As I stood in the hall outside.

And I caught the gist of a story there,

    As a mind's door opened wide.

A maid at her old typewriter,

    But I saw in her face a poem,

A gentle thought and a pensive sigh

    For a sight into future's gloam.

A wish, a hope to know the things

    That Fate for her had stored,

A sigh, a call for greater things

    To aid her strive the more.

To let her climb to nobler heights,

    To conquer, and to win

The finer gifts, the precious dole

    That to some hearts creep in.

I saw her scorn of commonness,

    And things of trifling class,

I read distaste for many sights

    She'd glimpsed along life's pass.

Ah there, I almost saw a tear

    Ere it was chased away,

A sorrow for one who had failed

    To play fair in love's day.

And now the shake of comely head,

    A smile is mustered brave,

No one but I had seen the poem,

    Had glimpsed a rhyme so grave.

I'd seen the petals of a soul,

    For a moment like a bloom

Toward the sunlight glad unfold

    And banish dreary gloom.

And as I trudged on down the hall,

    I breathed a simple prayer

For one who'd dreamed as I had dreamed

    About old Dame Fate's wares.

DEVINE

He's charge of the ward where I'm quartered,

    And justly he serves us each day,

Smoothing out tangles and troubles,

    Erasing pain out of our way.

Quiet and steady and kindly,

    He watches the lads in the line,

Knows them and guards them and helps them,

    This fellow that's known as Devine.

Sometimes when troubles seem mighty

    And you think that you haven't a friend,

When the world is all dark to your vision

    With problems almost without end,

He'll tackle your problem and solve it,

    With ease clear your eyes of their brine,

To him it's but everyday duty,

    This fellow that's known as Devine.

I've watched as some sick one was troubled,

    And distorted obsession took hold,

Then is his spirit seen plainest,

    As he wrestles with spirit grown bold.

And I've seen him bring peace to a patient

    Who was having a mighty tough time,

With success were his efforts rewarded,

    This fellow that's known as Devine.

Should I choose from amongst life's professions

    A career to do the most good

For trembling humans in misery

    And those who are ne'er understood,

I would strive to comfort the needy,

    The peace of the booster be mine,

As I banished the fear of the wearied,

    Like this fellow that's known as Devine.

ANGEL OF WHISPERING HOPE

Along the rambling walls the night nurse goes,

    With measured tread she makes her silent rounds

About the greystone manse where those repose

    Who waken, tremble at the slightest sound.

A careful glance at each white-covered bed,

    A chart consulted here, a record there.

On and on, yet not a word be said

    To rouse the ill ones resting from their cares.

Beside each white-clad bed she lingers still,

    And, perchance, breathes a hasty, fervent prayer.

A tender thought comes to the portals of her will,

    That someone's son, or brother, suffers there.

On down to where the gloomy sections yawn,

    Where hopeless ones must spend their wearied years.

For them, the nurse's smile: the only dawn

    To mix a shaft of gladness with their tears.

To Smith, who coughs away his other lung;

    To Jones, who fevered, gasps for one more drink;

To Brown, who his young life on liquor flung,

    She eases them, as they go o'er life's brink.

So, on and on, the guardian of the weak

    Treads on her way to ease the pain of souls,

To aid their cause, to help them try and seek

    The best in life. This is the nurse's goal.

Unpraised, unhallowed, unrewarded, she

    Like saintly lily brought to felon's pen,

She sends her heart and mind that some may see

    That peace can reign in a vale of passing men.

And many a wreck about to float off with the tide

    Would have passed on with just a mumbled curse,

Had there not been one watching at his side

    Who broadcast S. O. S. and signed off simply "Nurse."

Author's Note:

No patient can appreciate the work of a nurse as well as a mental patient.

SALUTATION AD INFINITUM

Where beckon stately, solemn age-wise oaks

    That guard old Greystone on its sky-flung hill,

There stands the haven, as though God hath spoke

    And ordered this great refuge for His ill.

Within the gloomy walls, the white-clad, tireless force

    That treat the brain and ease the troubled mind,

Go on their way to banish dread remorse,

    To bring the dawn and leave the dark behind.

It must be glory, seasoned with a dash of fame,

    To live careers that bring such peace to men.

To leave all else and play the thankless game

    Unsung by gifted bard,—so few to understand.

To list to senseless screams that wake the slumbering night,

    To hark to chilling moans that echo through the halls,

To toil 'mongst blazing brains that will not quiet.

    To patient be, nor weaken, twixt those ghostly walls,

Could but the ardent poet, who dreams of flowers and trees,

    Tarry awhile with us who dwell 'neath guarded ken,

A wondrous lyric he'd write, that fain would please

    The hearts of those whose loved ones stare from shrouded fens.

Could but the outer world of mankind cast their eyes

    O'er our quiet, restful ward, their foolish dread

Would fly, and truth present a glad surprise,

    For here no pain survives, but mercy rules instead.

For us no dismal cot, no darkened, murky room,

    No harsh-voiced keeper, with rattling, jangling keys

But sunlight, books and music are our boon,

    And human hearts can surely smile with these.

No sympathy we seek, no need have we

    That's not fulfilled, but you would please us well

If you would spread the deeds of those who help us see

    The shining trail to health, where we would dwell.

So to ye toilers in the white of mercy's garb

    Who bring us peace when trouble rends us wild

This uncouth rhyme is not by word-rich bard,

    But when you pass the Styx, then—God will smile.

CALLING

Oh mate, out there in the busy world,

    Can't you hear my call to you?

Can't you hear me whisper when twilight falls

    That I am needing you?

I need your voice when the shadows fall,

    I need your prayerful grace,

I need your memory near my heart,

    To help me win the race.

You must be somewhere out beyond

    These chilly, frowning bars,

I know you're there for I have read

    A promise in the stars.

And unknown pal, if I knew you

    Would say a little prayer

For me, 'twould ease a lonely heart

    That's so tired of its care.

I know that you are out there, pal.

    Your spirit must be nigh,

I hope that I shall find you, pal.

    Before I come to die.

I'm waiting here upon the hill,

    Eyes turned up toward the blue,

To wait God's great all-mercied will,

    To tell me what to do.

I once thought that 'twas just to die

    That I came to this place,

But now I see no reason why

    I should not join the race

Out in the busy, bustling world

    Where much work's to be done

By every human who will toil

    With peace till set of sun.

So some day I may meet you, girl,

    As round the world I roam,

And if so on a mystic isle

    We'll build a hallowed home.

And should you crave bright yellow gold,

    I'll shower you with much,

But, gee! I hope you do not pine

CALLING

For jewels, wealth and such.

For money's put me where I am,

    To me it's been a curse.

It's made me slave to poison rum,

    Drove me from bad to worse.

Ah, could I trade my gilded mine

    For life of disease free,

I'd leave the yellow muck behind,

    And toil eternally.

I hope to meet you, unknown pal,

    When the doctor's work is done.

And I can stride out in the world

    From the halls of North-Two-One.

WE PATIENTS WONDER

Oh Doctor, Doctor Curry,

    When the busy day has gone,

Don't you rest in peaceful slumber

    Till the crash of flowered dawn?

I wonder what you feel like,

    As you sit down on your bed,

And think of those you toil for

    In the vale of living dead.

Does a gentle wave of comfort

    Float down about you there,

As the thanks of grateful thousands

    Are wafted up in prayer?

You must be very sure

    Of a bright, eternal home,

Way up there with other workers

    Who have banished fear and groans.

WE PATIENTS WONDER

Don't you feel that God has picked you

From a million worthy sons,

To smooth away the misery

From his ailing, suffering ones?

As you float in gentle slumber

Does a murmur fill the air,

As of grateful mortals' voices

Sending songs to drown your cares?

And when you wake and rustle

In the gentle smile of morn

Do you hear a benediction

Like the sound from golden horns?

Rest in peace, oh, Marcus Curry,

We your subjects wish you well,

Though our tongues be numb and helpless

Still our thoughts our message tells.

THAT'S SCOTTY

Slowly walking down the street,

Dignified and always neat,

Unburdened heart and honest feet—

> That's Scotty.

Not in flashy, sporty car,

She would rather walk by far

Than to have her conscience marred—

> That's Scotty.

With her even, artless walk,

And her burring Gaelic talk!

Lily fair on high, proud stalk—

> That's Scotty.

Always greets you with a smile

That stays with you for many a mile,

With conversation out of style—

> That's Scotty.

THAT'S SCOTTY

Walk on, Scotty, there are few

Who are spoken of as true.

We must lift our hats to you.

       Hurrah for Scotty!

Opening Of The Shell

I leave my shell and step from my cocoon

    I blink and stretch and yawn, a flowered world

Is all about, the yellow wealth of goldenrod that blooms

    Close to a gorgeous purple aster's curls.

Half fearful, I peer out at new gay life,

    But faith returns, for here close at my side

Other cocoons open to face the same new strife

    Other wakened ones prepare to breast life's tide.

Our tree where we have slept protected from all things,

    Rocked, cared for, held secure by waving boughs,

Now bids us soar away in joy to sing,

    To statesman be, or follow humble plow.

GREETINGS TO
GOVERNOR LARSON

Greetings, honored chief of glorious state:

    We welcome you with dim but grateful eyes.

We're glad that in the outer world there wait

    True friends who work for us, and with surprise

You'll gaze when you see how we patients know

    That you are to your emblems always fair,

That you have harkened to all human woes

    And steered our stately vessel "on the square."

And to you, chieftain of this great and sovereign state,

    Of justice, and of mercy's rightful fame,

I say that up above a wreath there waits

    For him who aids the sick ones in life's game.

Look out amongst our trembling heads and see

    The wonders that by science for us are done;

The care and Occupational Therapy

That's granted us great succor, one by one.

I say to you, oh, statesman who has heeded orphans' pleas,

    Who heard the hungry mother's whisper thru' the night,

That could you know their joy your hectored heart would cease

    Its duller moments, and your soul would revel at the sight.

On, Morgan Larson, on up the curbing lanes,

    Where guiltless humans seek thy aid divine,

Stride on, still heading eastward, e'er destroying pain,

    And bidding hearts be glad that till you came had pined.

Our doctors here are striving 'gainst great odds

    To heal our sore, bruised minds as best they may.

Thy hand to them will further work of God.

    Give ear to them: they're with you all the way.

Author's Note:

Composed as a greeting to Governer Larson, for the patients of Greystone Park, to show their appreciation of the care and treatment granted them by the State.

And Last

Now my rhymes are finished,

    I send this book of blue

Out amongst you mortals

    And hope I've brought to you

An hour or so of pleasure,

    And given a little time

Of interest and forgetfulness

    With these crude rambling rhymes.

And in this rhyme rough-metred

    I'm bidding you good-bye,

I'm leaving dear old Greystone,

    Once more with Fate to vie.

I'm going out into the world;

    The doctors say I'm well.

Oh, what a gloried message

    A broken one to tell.

I'm going to the work I love,

    To doctor ailing trees,

To garb drab hills with foliage

    And cool the summer's breeze.

I'm going to swing my sweating lads

    On through a marble hill,

And listen to the grind of gears,

    And song of sledge and drill.

I'm going back to making dams

    And building great, wide parks,

Where humans tired of city's din

    May hear the trill of larks.

I shall toil 'mongst friendly giants

    Who beckon in the breeze,

I shall use the verdant knowledge

    Luther Burbank gave to me.

I'm going to slay Jap beetles,

    Rout the Mediterranean fly,

Spray with poison harmful insects,

    And watch corn borers die.

For twenty years I've worked with trees,

    And garnered much success,

Till I dabbled with the sporting fools

AND LAST

And woke up one possessed.

But they've treated me and straightened

A lot of untried lines,

I'm master of my vessel now,

And confident my mind.

And now as I bid you good-bye,

I only want to add

That you who've liked my writings

Have made me mighty glad.

You've granted many happy hours

To this health-endowing hill,

And helped some fighting men to build

A strong, unswerving will.

Good-bye, my friends; Greystone, farewell.

You've brought great good to me.

May you help others break their spell.

Good-bye, all.—R. D. C.

MY SOJOURN AT
GREYSTONE PARK BY R.D.C

In this brief history of my experience in the New Jersey State Hospital at Greystone Park, I chronicle my own impressions and ideas.

The thought struck me that perhaps a certain amount of good might be accomplished were I to depict life here at the great hospital as it really is and not with the blind, misunderstood views of someone writing of what they have only been told.

This is written in my own way, with no help nor suggestions from anyone. I have asked several doctors who are executives here about the advisability of adding to my rhymes the history of my sojourn here but they were non-committal, not wishing to be quoted in any way other than that it would be fine could only the public know of the real rehabilitation work done here and at the same time lose their centuries old dread and fear of anything that remotely suggests an insane asylum.

I would like to help banish the trembling, the fear and the dread of the parents, relatives and loved ones of my brother and sister patients. I have observed so many visitors of patients here and so many of them are actually cold with apprehension at what may happen within our gates, Ah, could I give my worthless life to remove the pitiful, sobbing look in the eyes of so many mothers, sisters and friends when they walk down the hallways and bid their loved ones goodbye. Sometimes I wanted to rush up to some party who had entirely the wrong idea of Greystone and yell: "You are wrong: we have no dungeons here. We have no handcuffs, no chains, nor cold, clammy cells to add to humanity's suffering. We are helping humanity. We remove their suffering all we can. Let me tell you the truth about this place."

But alas, I am only a patient and it is not my place to approach strangers, for so many would not understand. And because I wish the friend or relative of every single patient beneath these great, merciful spires to know the real Greystone Park, I am dedicating this, my first literary contribution, to the public. It has plenty of flaws. But then this love for writing has come upon me suddenly. I never knew that I could write anything that people would like to read until Greystone Park put me through its cleaner.

I have been in the horticultural game for years and like it a great deal. My greatest pleasure, before I was treated here, was to work with trees and plants. I have made quite an extraordinary success in the propagation of plant and vegetable life, it is true, but never in all my life have I enjoyed anything as I have just scribbling my poor rhymes and stories for the patients of this hospital and their relatives.

When the treatments were started here, writing was one of the most remote things from my mind.

I wish I might take everyone of the outer world through Greystone Park. It would drive away every particle of fear or dread of a mental institution.

From ·the oatmeal, hash, bread and butter,—butter, not oleo-margarine, and coffee at breakfast in the morning to the cozy, warm, well ventilated rooms, or dormitories in which we sleep, there is found and felt the spirit of careful consideration for the health of the patient.

We are out for long walks every single day that the weather permits, and in spring, summer and fall the grass beneath the shade trees is literally covered with patients, while others are loitering along the roads out amongst the woods with their attendants.

Some people think we are sad here. Quite the contrary, I assure you. Everything is given to us that can be given to make life brighter for us; we have long moving pictures every second week, we have a dance with splendid music every week, and periodically there are parties with music, games and refreshments.

We have as good an orchestra of all pieces as one could desire which, through the days, plays on the wards for the benefit of those patients who are unable to go to the shows, parties and dances.

As for the attention each patient receives I will state that it is a system difficult to improve upon. Each ward has from two to six attendants, one being placed in direct charge to make reports to doctors and supervisors.

Every few hours a supervisor walks through the ward looking over the patients and inquiring about the general welfare. A doctor makes the rounds twice daily or oftener, and any patient ailing in any way is prescribed for accordingly:

Everything is done to win our confidence. From time to time the patients are brought before the general staff, the members of which study the history of the case, and when the patient has recovered to the extent of being able, this body of trained psychiatrists decide upon parole and later his discharge.

The world should know of the indescribable good wrought here at Greystone Park. I wish I might give my life to the cause for which Dr. Marcus A. Curry and Dr. George B. McMurray are striving.

I have traveled the whole world, mixed with every type of human, and the divers associations have developed within me a reliable instinct which tells me plainly of sincerity and unselfishness, or indifference and greed, and I tell you readers, that in thirty years of travel never have I met with men who have gained one-half the good for humanity that these two men have brought about.

If you would have told me those first months of my sojourn here that I would be writing poetry and stories that anyone would like to read in two months' time, I would have walked away wondering which one of us two was the crazier.

I was worried, fearful of everything and everybody, I thought that the doctors were planning to kill me. I feverishly inquired about the padded cells, the Oregon boots and the straight jacket. There didn't seem to be any. Not one of the patients in ward four of the Reception had seen them. But still I stewed and fretted. I don't know what I did for quite awhile. But I've been told plenty, and if even half of what I am said to have done is true I must have been some pest.

The first thing that happened to me upon entering the Reception Building was to get a hot shower bath. Then I was dressed in soft, spongy pajamas, bathrobe and slippers and put to bed in a comfy, light room with windows wide open and everything spotlessly white and clean. Should I desire water or anything of the kind there were attendants constantly in the hall only a few feet from my door to attend to my wants.

Now there was one thing about the entry business that lots of people might not like and that was to stay in bed for three days on a liquid diet. It seemed rather hard at the time but I can readily see now that the complete rest, both for stomach and brain was a wonderful thing.

After the three days I was given my own apparel, which in the meantime had been fumigated, and I was turned out with several other patients to smoke, read and to walk about in the sun-parlor, or to do whatever I pleased, always, of course, under constant observation. This is a very exceptional feature of this hospital. It is by means of this observation that many of the types are differentiated. For instance, should a patient be depressed or melancholy, if he is possessed with suicidal ideas the fact is soon known, and he is watched and protected from injuring himself.

The mental examination, as well as the physical, is an intensive one here. There is a separate corps of psychiatrists for this work, each with a secretary, and during the examination, which is really an old fashioned talk, with the patient as much at his ease as possible, every word, every look, every expression and action, normal and abnormal, is written down and added to the history of the case. This means everything to accomplish the patients' recovery, as once the medical staff knows enough concerning a case to give a diagnosis they go right to work on the type of treatment covering his particular need.

There is no guess work. It is not tolerated. The doctors of the medical staff demand that the examining physician and alienist submit a clear written record of the findings of the case at the time the patient is brought before them to discuss and arrive at a diagnosis. I shall not attempt to depict my sensations while at the Reception Building. It is too vague, some of it. In fact, most of it is twisted and indistinct, and I wasn't myself there, as I am now. I was pretty sick, I guess. But one thing I can remember about it—— "The Fear." That hellish, grizzly Fear. Yet I don't know what it was. I don't know what I was afraid of. I am not going to try and write about it. Things ran together. But two doctors I am going to bring into the chronicle here. They are two men who were good to me, gave me a break. I could talk to them. They didn't seem to notice my erratic talk. They didn't appear to see my jumpy, broken gestures. They gave me a square deal all the way. So did the others as far as that goes, especially that body of sincere medicos and psychiatrists who compose the finest staff of any hospital in the world, bar none, who ever congregated to diagnose the case of a patient.

I've known many doctors who were thoughtful and serious, but never have I met a group as thorough, as courteous, and as thoughtful as the one I was summoned before here.

But I am getting away from my story.

The two doctors who won my confidence and faith were doctors Gebertig, in the Reception, and Laatsch, in the Clinic Building. They told me the whole truth, their honest opinion of my case. They pointed out what might be done to help me. They showed me where my cooperation would further my case greatly. They didn't paint me a picture of roses and white lace. They gave me facts and they never told me a lie. I trusted them and I started to mend.

I was transferred to Ward Four of the same building. Now for the sake of some of you people who think of asylums or hospitals in the terms of steel and torture, let me describe ward Four. First, it is immense. Next, it is blamed near all windows—and get ready to call me a liar now, tho' I'm not—NO BARS. Not a single bar on a window or door. No, I do not mean that one can get woozy all of a sudden and jump through a window and kill himself. Oh no, but there is only a heavy screen over the windows. The walls have a window about every two feet as an average and most places there are double and triple windows. So much for the fresh air and sunshine. Now comes the parlor or lounging room. Its furnishings consist of a piano, radio, two couches, comfortable easy chairs, two long polished tables, books, magazines, papers of almost every description. Rugs on the floor and curtains at the windows, everything clean, really clean, if you please. Then there is the smoking room, also comfortably furnished. There is not a dark, damp corner in the whole place. So if you have a relative or friend in the Reception Building pray have no fear for his fresh air, sunshine and clean quarters. He'll have them plenty.

Now, I shall show you as well as I can with my untutored efforts a room in which things happened as nearly of a miraculous nature as any I have ever seen or heard. It is the "fountain of a thousand wonders", the Hydro Therapy Ward. Good natured Doc. White is there in charge and has for his assistant the cleanest-cut, upstanding, upright, most sincere young Irishman that ever picked a "pratie" or harked for the note of the banshee.

It's I who know what those two chaps are doing for the world. I sat there and watched young lads and old men ailing and miserable, baked and steamed in cabinets day after day until they were granted strength and peace and quiet nerves by that almost uncanny treatment that has so great a part in the work of regained health.

And believe me, friend, when I say that never have I seen any two mortals any more persevering, or kind, or patient with those upon whom they toil than Doc. White and Bill Moran in the "Hydro". I mean just that. They have done much for me.

I was transferred to the Main Building in the fall and at my own request I was put with the greenhouse force under Mr. Otto Koch. The greenhouse is one unit of the splendid Occupational Therapy Dept. Out in the fresh mountain air I thrived greatly. There was no specified work for me to do. The object that the doctors wanted to be attained was mind interest. They wanted me to forget myself and my own supposed trouble.

It began to work and I actually thought myself getting better. Of course I was taking regular treatment—high power injections each week—but the trust placed in me, the fact that I knew the Doctors wanted to help me was big, big factor, you can bet on that.

And then it happened, presto, like that. The chap who had held the Patient Editor's chair in the office of "The Psychogram", which is our Hospital organ, was not there to write an editorial, and for some reason or other—I never knew how he came to pick me—Dr. McMurray asked me to write the story. I do not think I shall ever forget the few minutes following this question as to whether I could write. I had never written anything worthwhile. For an instant, I was confused. Then he looked straight at me, as only Dr. George B. McMurray can look, and something started at my very toes and coursed right to my temples. "You can write," some invisible, wordless message came to me. I do not understand what it was nor have I ever asked, but friends, out there in your great, glistening world of freedom, from that moment words rushed from my pen in rhyme. I wrote the editorial; it pleased him. From that moment, I was another person. I hadn't cared much for life up to then but now I was crazy to live. Then in just a few days he placed me in the Print Shop as Manager of "The Psychogram". He gave me a clear rein. He trusted me. He gave me a parole with no restrictions and gave me no orders nor threats.

From then on, I thought of little else but "The Psychogram" and Dr. McMurray. I saw that he was trying to help me and I knew that he was going to try and put me back on my feet again. He trusted me. Good folks, can you imagine what that meant? I wanted to start down the road as fast as I could tear. I was still afraid, not well yet by a long sight. I didn't know him then as I do now. I wanted to leave the noise and the shuffling feet and the sadness.

But I didn't go. I wonder why? There was the open road. There were plenty of trains and automobiles. I used to go and come as I wished. But, well, whatever it was that held me, it was stronger by a thousand times than my desire to leave, for I stayed and things righted themselves a little at a time. Slowly and surely, something had gripped me, something that I knew nothing about then. But I know now. For the first time in years and years I am living right, thinking right and know that I shall always be right, because of the confidence, the faith, the patient help of the doctors of Greystone Park am I able to take my place in the world as a producer, not a spoiler, whether the place be here between these great merciful walls, or elsewhere.

Thanks to Greystone Park I can compose and write things that people like to read. I couldn't do it before I came here. I am not well yet. I still have my disturbances occasionally. But they are rare now. I am progressing. I can control my temper, but I am nervous, although that has been reduced to a minimum. It isn't done in a day. Many young folks I know now think cures come easy. Fools, such fools! Yet I said the same once long ago. But one has a difficult time trying to educate the youth of today or any day. They must learn and suffer and moan. All of us must do a little of that, I guess.

I have done mighty little good for the world of humanity. Now Dr. Curry, Dr. McMurray, and all the doctors in whose charge I have been have granted me the strength and health and desire to give my best to the world. I didn't think I was worth salvaging. I know I am now, and if when the medical staff call me before them and decide that it is better for me within this institution, I can smile with a great smile. For there is my 15-page messenger, "The Psychogram" and there are people who like to read the rhymes of my heart, perhaps some poor soul on the slow, tedious road to recovery may read one of my rhymes with the hope that is depicted in its lines, and perhaps he shall gaze out through the bars and glimpse a gay world beyond, and smile, and if so, well is the life of R. D. C. repaid for its lengthy sojourn, even though it be unto death. For I have learned much of good here at Greystone Park.

While here I have found the friendship of one who believes that I have the ability to do some splendid things in the world in spite of the years which I have wasted. And became that friend, who has always lived a noble, upright life, has faith in me I cannot fail to succeed in the great design I have laid out for my future life's actions.

And now, my unseen friends. I must bring this to a close. I wish I could have written more convincingly and connectedly of the first six months of my stay here, but someway it's hazy, sort of run together and indistinct. I am dazed at this new, glorified life. I am a little uncertain, a little afraid, just as I imagine an insect feels as it emerges from the cocoon on a balmy spring day and looks out upon a world of dazzling brilliancy and floral grandeur. And as the butterfly emanates from the cocoon I have emerged from the shell of darkness and sordidness and stand looking out into a joyous world of normalcy and achievement.

ABOUT THE PRESENTERS

Sherri is the daughter of Kani and Dr. Jacob Forman, DDS. Dr. Forman served in the dental clinic of the old Greystone Park Hospital, from April 1960, until his untimely death in April 1972. He also served as a dentist in the US Army in the Pacific Theatre during WW II, retiring as a Lieutenant Colonel in 1968. Sherri is a veteran of the US Air Force and after leaving the service, earned an MS in psychology at Auburn University at Montgomery, Alabama. Her master's thesis, "Personality as Predictor of Adjustment in Military Sojourners," was published in 2001, in *Military Psychology*, a journal of the American Psychological Association. Sherri served as a *Consortium Research Fellow* at the US Army Research Institute for the Behavioral & Social Sciences at Fort Benning, Georgia, during her doctoral program internship in Applied Psychology, at the University of Georgia. She also served as an adjunct instructor of psychology, Fayetteville Technical Community College, Fort Bragg, North Carolina.

Stephen served in the British Royal Navy Submarine Service and studied history at Fayetteville State University, North Carolina. Stephen and Sherri recently published, *King Alfred's Middle Earth — Books Most Necessary to Know*.

47756006R00163

Made in the USA
Middletown, DE
01 September 2017